"THE EARTH CHARTER"
A STUDY BOOK OF
REFLECTION FOR ACTION

ELISABETH M. FERRERO, PH.D.

&

JOE HOLLAND, PH.D.

Published in Cooperation with
The International Consortium of Religion & Ecology
Pax Romana/Catholic Movement for Intellectual & Cultural Affairs USA
The Florida Council of Catholic Scholarship

REDWOODS PRESS
The Redwoods Institute
A Project of EcoWorks, Inc.
Website: www.RedwoodsInstitute.com
Email: contact@RedwoodsInstitute.com

For Dan, Eugenia, Natanya, Scott, and Seth,
and for all the young leaders of the world
who are called to pioneer the creation of
a fresh and healing ecological civilization

Printed in the United States by
Redwoods Press

E A N 1 3   9 7 8 - 0 9 7 6 3 5 8 0 0 8
I S B N   0 - 9 7 6 3 5 8 0 - 0 - X
G F 4 7   . F 4 7   2 0 0 5

2008-07-11

TABLE OF CONTENTS

THE FOUR BROAD PRINCIPLES

OF THE EARTH CHARTER

I.

Respect and Care for the Community of Life

II.

Ecological Integrity

III.

Social and Economic Justice

IV.

Democracy, Nonviolence, and Peace

1

Executive Director
Earth Charter International Secretariat
San José, Costa Rica

T here are futurists and scientists who question our very survival, if civilization is unable to come to terms with its social, environmental, and cultural challenges. I do not believe seeking merely survival will save us or unveil the joy and richness inherent in Creation. I believe that what humanity faces is to again recognize, and dwell, in connectivity with the perpetual, and to ensure its existence and its evolutionary unfolding.

The sea is where I met the perpetual as it greeted me with its spray that never ceased to enliven, and calmed with incessant sounds and rolling motion that I experienced as a lullaby from and with God. The sea was infinitely larger than me; it was forever; and it was where I met with and communicated with the transcendent. I sense overwhelming connection, the air, water, living beings and the universe. However, where there was once reoccurring cycles of expansive birth and creation, there are now thoughts of despoliation and looming doubts of future degradation. We cannot experience inner peace if our neighbors are in conflict. Our food is not easy to digest if our neighbor does not have the food to keep him alive and healthy. Social injustices and environment degradation are interconnected with the other challenges, such as achieving an ethical political and economic system. Here lies the need for an integrated approach to address our current situation and it is here the Earth Charter is offered as an answer.

"THE EARTH CHARTER" - A STUDY BOOK OF REFLECTION FOR ACTION is a very timely instrument, offered as a tool for the many groups that have begun teaching about the Earth Charter. News of this momentous and laborious contribution came unbidden. This deep reflection on the Earth Charter by Elizabeth Ferrero and Joe Holland places the Earth Charter in historical and spiritual perspective and I believe it will be read not only "reflectively", but also as a call to action. Such love of labor as is evidenced in this publication connects not only the authors with our Secretariat; it connects the readers with us also. This connectivity is quite like what I experienced by the sea, and will again experience, joined with all of you.

MIRIAN VILELA

Earth Charter International Secretariat
San José, Costa Rica
www.earthcharter.org

GREETINGS FROM
MSGR. FRANKLYN M. CASALE

President
Saint Thomas University,
Miami, Florida, USA

T his important publication, "THE EARTH CHARTER" -
A STUDY BOOK OF REFLECTION FOR ACTION, repre-
sents an intellectual contribution from scholars at St. Thomas
University to the growing global ecological movement. The
guide is co-authored by two of our distinguished professors,
Dr. Elisabeth Ferrero and Dr. Joe Holland.

Encouraged by Pope John Paul II's 1991 *World Peace Day
Statement*, we, as a Catholic University have committed ourselves to a sustainable future. We are proud to join with the
Catholic Bishops around the around world who have height-
ened awareness by issuing more than 80 pastoral letters on
ecology. The issue however does not limit itself to the pur-
view of the Catholic Church. Similar statements have come
from countless other world religious leaders.

St. Thomas University has been promoting a fresh ecological
consciousness for all of society. Dr. Ferrero and Dr. Holland
have been deeply involved in the issue for years. They have
led our University for more than a decade now in pioneering
the introduction of ecological content across the campuses
and in the academic curriculum.

In 1992, in recognition of our pioneering efforts, our University was selected from over 1600 applicants nationwide by 28
of the leading environmental organizations in the United

States to receive the prestigious *Renew America Environmental Achievement Award.* Dr. Ferrero also has been a primary organizer of a series of conferences on Spirituality and Sustainability in Assisi, Italy. As awareness grows at the global level the amount of commitment from our University increases and the attention to the Earth Charter gives us a new opportunity to put ourselves at the service of the issue.

"We stand at a critical moment in Earth's history, a time when humanity must choose its future" (first sentence of Preamble to the Earth Charter). As our planetary society faces increasing ecological threats, all sectors of society – universities, religions, governments, businesses – need to join to ensure an ecologically sustainable future for the children of coming generations. Hopefully, this new book by Professors Ferrero and Holland will be of valuable service in the call to a future based on ecological sustainability.

The concern with the ecology by the worldwide Catholic community, and here specifically support for the Earth Charter, may be seen as part of the Catholic tradition's "consistent ethic of life," which opposes abortion, euthanasia, the death penalty, and all violations of human dignity. The growing Catholic concern with ecology, while maintaining the preeminent dignity of human life, reflects our awareness that human life is in turn part of a wider matrix or biosphere of life, which is also part of God's splendid creation.

It was in this sense that recently Cardinal Oscar Andres Rodriguez Maradiaga of Honduras made the following statement:

Facing the World Summit on Sustainable Development in the year 2002, we urge all governments to support the Earth Charter through the United Nations General Assembly so that the care for the environment, the common good and respect for life serve as fun-

*damental basis for sustainable development within the globaliza-
tion of solidarity.* (July 12, 2001)

In addition, I take pleasure in noting the warm and supportive greeting sent on behalf of Pope John Paul II to Mr. Mikhail Gorbachev regarding his work on the Earth Charter:

*To his Excellency Monsignor Angelo Comatri, Pontifical Dele-
gate. Having been notified that Mr. Mikhail Gorbachev, the distinguished President of Green Cross International, is in Italy to
present the project of the Earth Charter, the Supreme Pontiff re-
quests your Excellency to express his satisfaction for a work well
done in defending our environmental heritage, and to encourage this
esteemed statesman's meritorious effort to bring forth greater respect
for the planet's resources, given by God so that every person may
live a dignified life. His Holiness sends his greeting and blessing.
(Signed) Archbishop Leonardo Sandri, Sostituto, Secretariat of
State, Vatican City State.*

*(Free translation by Elisabeth Ferrero and Joe Holland from
original telegram sent by Archbishop Sandri on the occasion of Mr.
Gorbachev's presentation of the Earth Charter in Urbino, Italy on
2 July 2001.)*

It is our hope that this study guide will reinforce in local
communities as well as in academia itself the commitment to
make the Earth Charter a living document for our age.

REV. MONSIGNOR FRANKLYN M. CASALE

St. Thomas University
Miami, Florida USA
www.stu.edu

ELISABETH M. FERRERO. *Elisabeth is Professor of Humanities at Saint Thomas University in Miami, Florida, USA. She holds an M.A. and a Ph.D. from Rutgers University in New Jersey. Closely involved with the Earth Charter process since 1998, Elisabeth produced the official Italian translation of Draft II of the Earth Charter and was appointed by the Earth Council to start the National Committee of the Earth Charter in Italy. She founded the St. Thomas University Study Abroad for Earth (SAFE) program, which has organized ecological study programs in Italy and Ecuador. For many years, she organized major conferences in Assisi, Italy on Ecology and Spirituality. She is also a published poet in both Italian and English. Elisabeth, a devoted disciple and close friend of Thomas Berry, is the President of EcoWorks, Inc. a not-for-profit organization devoted to social and environmental justice.*

JOE HOLLAND. *Joe is Professor of Philosophy & Religion at Saint Thomas University in Miami, Florida, US. He holds an M.A. and Ph.D. from the University of Chicago, and has studied at the New School in New York City, Niagara University, the Universidad Católica in Ponce, Puerto Rico, and the Universidad Católica in Santiago, Chile. He is President of the US intellectual and professional Federation of Pax Romana/International Catholic Movement on Intellectual and Cultural Affairs, as well as Coordinator of the Florida Council of Catholic Scholarship. Joe has published eight books and countless articles. His book with Peter Henriot, SOCIAL ANALYSIS, has been translated into six languages and is used in schools and by grass-roots groups across the world. His most recent book is MODERN CATHOLIC SOCIAL TEACHING.*

AUTHORS' ACKNOWLEDGEMENTS

There are so many wonderful people to thank! Without learning from their wisdom and being inspired by their vision, we never would have been able to write this small book.

First and foremost, we offer our deep gratitude to the many people in the wider Earth-Charter movement, for they too have been our teachers, mentors, and often friends. Here we think especially of Mirian Vilela, Rick Clugston, Steven Rockefeller, Peter Adriance, Marina Bakhnova, Lisa Bardack, Johannah Bernstein, Harold Bradley, Colonel Franco Caldari, Giuliano Cannata, Donald Cashen, Kamla Chowdhry, Adriano Ciani, Anthony Cortese, Severn Cullis-Suzuki, Yutaka Furuta, Moacir Gadotti, John A. Grim, Wakako Hironaka, John A. Hoyt, Yolanda Kakabadse, Rustem Khairov, Roger W. Koment, Pamela Kraft, Christian Leipert, Christina Liamzon, Alexander Likhotal, Rudd Lubbers, Finn Lynge, Wangari Maathai, Brandan Mackey, Jay McDaniels, Rev. Peter Damian Massengill, Frank Meyberg, Patricia Morales, Rev. Max Mizzi, Countess Paolozzi, Teresa Africa Perez, Giuseppe Ratti, Tamra Raven, Jan Roberts, Thomas Rogers, Mohamed Sahnoun, M. A. Partha Sarathy, Karl-Ludwig Schibel, Mercedes Sosa, Charles Spencer, Maurice Strong, Enzo Tiezzi, Amadou Toumani Touré, Mary Evelyn Tucker, Frederick S. vom Saal, Stefano Parmigiani, Jacqueline Wagner, and in a special way the late Vittorio Falsina and Maximo Kalaw.

Also with deep fondness, our gratitude goes to Thomas Berry, geologian and cultural-religious historian, visionary genius, and our teacher, mentor, and friend. He, more than anyone we know, has been a lyrical pioneer in exploring the new stage of human consciousness in the ecological era. We thank also Brian Swimme, astrophysicist, colleague, and friend, who has worked so closely with Tom in articulating the new vision, making his own contribution to it, and bringing it to broad audiences in a style filled with poetry and depth. In particular we thank Rick Clugston, James Conley, Constantine Kalogeras, Steve Smith, Claire Wilson, and Maureen Holland for proofreading the manuscript. . Our special thanks of appreciation go to Wolfgang Riesterer for his invaluable technological and electronic expertise.

We thank the many people at St. Thomas University, where we both have been teaching for many years now. The whole university community has provided a warm and encouraging family spirit. We wish we could name everyone but must limit ourselves to only a few. So we offer a special word of thanks to our President, Msgr. Franklyn Casale, as well as to past and present academic leadership including Richard Greene, Norma Goonen, Gary McCloskey, Gregory Chan, Pamela Cingel, Fred Holman, Joseph Iannone, Mercedes Iannone, Susan Angulo, James Conley, and Gary Feinberg. We also thank our colleague in Philosophy, Olga Huchingson, and her spouse James Huchingson, as well as all our departmental colleagues and friends, namely Andrea Campbell, Barbara Graham, Rafael Montes, Richard Raleigh, Philip Reckford, Gloria Ruiz, Jorge Sardiñas, Philip Shepardson, and Marene Clarke. In addition, a word of thanks to other colleagues and friends at St. Thomas and elsewhere who in some special way have also been supportive of ecology and/or this project, namely Rev. Ed Blackwell, Bryan Cooper, Helen Jacobstein, Francis Sicius, Mark Wolff, Constantine Kalogeras, Craig Reese, and Mark Rogers.

We also wish to thank our colleagues in the worldwide Pax Romana family, since Pax Romana / CMICA-USA is a co-sponsor of this project. In particularly we thank the Kirchner family, founders and long time sustainers of the movement, particularly the late Ed Kirchner, Louisa Kirchner, and Joe Kirchner, as well as the international leadership of Anselmo Lee, Patricio Rodé, Paul Ortega, and Antoine Sontag, and particularly the Coordinator of the Pax Romana International Working Group on Ecology, Teresa Mourad, and especially for her assistance with the study session at the end of the book. We especially remember the late Supee Nuchanart (Noi) of Bangkok, Thailand. Supee, who was Pax Romana Vice President for Asia from 1995 to 2000 and also a university professor of Biology, vigorously and warmly promoted ecological consciousness throughout the movement.

Lastly we offer a special word of thanks to many family and friends and especially those in the wider ecology movement and in religious movements supporting ecology. Here we think especially of Rev. Donald Conroy, President of the International Consortium on Religion and Ecology (ICORE), and D. Michael McCarron, Executive Director of the Florida Catholic Conference, which has inspired the Florida Council of Catholic Scholarship (FCCS). Both the ICORE and the FCCS are co-sponsors of this publication. We also think warmly of Eugenia Ferrero, Lori Bembanaste, James Collins, Paolo Diotallevi, Rev. Alfred Fritsch SJ, Todd Garland, Ana-Christina Gonzalez, Rev. James Gaughan, Rev. Michael Gillgannon, Marcia Guerrero, Paquita and Dan, and Natanya Holland, Walter Hubbard, Marcus and Glenda Keyes,

Marlene Lauritzen, Nerry Louis, Ferdinand and Robin Mahfoud, Mirian Teresa McGillis, Sr. Joan Mury MM., Bill Nichols, Rev. Patrick O'Neill, Rodney Petersen, Giovanni Principato, Frank Rogers, Zulma Ruiz, Selwyn Spanner, McGregor Smith, Rev. Robert Tagliaferri, Dwight E. Thompson, the late Msgr. Bryan Walsh, and Carole Warren.

All these wonderful people and so many more have been to us a constant inspiration, and we give them our warmest gratitude. Any errors, of course, are only our own.

THOMAS BERRY

Professor Emeritus, Fordham University
Cultural Historian and Ecological Visionary
Greensboro, North Carolina, USA

W e might think of the Earth Charter as perhaps the
most comprehensive document ever to be proposed
for approval by the United Nations Assembly. We are not
accustomed to think of ourselves as a component within the
larger community of Earth as envisaged by this Charter. Nor
have we considered that the well-being of the other components of Earth is a condition, not simply for our own human
well-being, but even for our survival.

We thought that we had accomplished something wonderful
when, at the end of World War II, we formed the United
Nations. Indeed it was an accomplishment to be fully appreciated after the collapse of the earlier League of Nations. Yet
it took the devastation of World War II, when, it is said, fifty
million people died, to bring the community of nations together in a formal organization.

It was almost in desperation that the Charter for the United
Nations was signed by 51 nations in October of 1945. Its
primary purpose was to maintain peace among the nations
and to increase cooperation in various fields of human activity, especially in economic, social, and cultural affairs. Here

was a context in which future conflicts that would arise between the nations could be mediated. The nations were determined that never again would such a conflict as that of the Great War occur within the human family.

With all its limitations and with all the conflicts that have arisen in these intervening years, the United Nations has fulfilled its role with remarkable success. It has enabled more than a hundred new nations to come into being and to take their place in the Assembly of Nations. As of the year 2001, the Assembly was composed of 189 members.

Among its more impressive achievements, the Assembly has asserted the Universal Declaration of Human Rights against the tyrannies and oppressions that peoples of the world have been enduring down through the centuries. Yet we find no rights and no protections offered for Earth against the tyrannies of the human.

It is against this background that we must envisage the Earth Charter, a document that was initiated within the Assembly of the United Nations at its meeting in Rio in 1992. Now, after almost ten years of discussion and rewriting, we look forward with enthusiasm to approval of the Charter. Just as the Charter of the United Nations itself was born out of a convulsive moment in human history, so the Earth Charter has come into being at a moment when the industrial period in human development has become so devastating to the sources of human survival that we find ourselves threatened in our continued existence on this planet. We are told by E. O. Wilson that the present extinction of living species is on a scale unequalled in the past 65 million years in the geobiological history of Earth.

We begin to recognize the arrogance of our view of Earth as primarily a *Natural Resource* to be used, rather than as an *Intimate Presence* to evoke that wonder and beauty, that healing and inspiration that is the fulfillment of our inner world. The natural world does indeed feed, clothe, and shelter us physically. Yet if we look to Earth simply as a resource to be exploited for its monetary value as well as for our human comfort and convenience, we will end up with a planet severely damaged in its life-giving capacities.

We need to understand that Earth in its primordial condition nourishes us in our inner spirit even while it provides for our physical needs. Here in the United States of America we have been oblivious of the damage that we have been doing by our relentless exploitation of Earth throughout the 20th century. We have been entranced with ourselves and our amazing inventions.

We seem not to realize the consequences of our move in the 1880's from an *organic, ever-renewing, land-based* economy, to an *extractive, non-renewing, industrial* economy. This was the critical moment. We must now move back from a non-renewing economy, dependent largely on limited petroleum-based energies, to an ever-renewing economy based on renewable energies of the natural world. Only if we take care of Earth, can Earth take care of us.

We begin to realize that Earth is a *communion of subjects,* not a *collection of objects.* Only an organic, ever-renewing, land-based economy can sustain itself and the planet where we dwell. This inner bonding of the human with the other components of Earth is what makes Earth, with both its human and its other-than-human components, a single integral community, a community that will live or die, prosper or be impoverished together. There is abundant room for human technologies but only for those that are coherent with Earth technologies. There can be no future for a civilization that bases itself on technologies that plunder Earth.

Even the deep pathos of our social inequalities can be remedied only with this integrity of the entire Earth community. Apart from the fertility of Earth we have no other source for our nourishment. Apart from the atmosphere that surrounds us we have no source for our breathing. Apart from the waters that flow in our streams and rivers, waters that flow up from the springs, waters from the deep aquifers within Earth; apart from these waters we have no refreshing water to drink or to sustain our cultivation of the land.

So too for the inner world of mind, imagination, and emotions. These faculties can be activated only through the wonders that we observe through our senses. If we lived on the moon our minds would be as empty as the moon, our imagination would be as limited as the lunar landscape, our emotions would be unfulfilled. The real reason why we cannot live on the Moon, on Mars, or any other planet, is that our inner world would shrivel within itself for lack of a wonder to commune with such as we find here on Earth.

These reflections reveal the need we have for the immense variety of experiences that we have here on this planet. They reveal also the self-destruction that occurs when we devastate the very sources of our life. To preserve this planet in its awesome majesty enables our small self to experience its fulfillment in our Great Self, the planet Earth, and beyond the Universe that reveals itself to us in all its grandeur out of the dark night skies.

FOREWORD

RICHARD M. CLUGSTON

Executive Director
Center for Respect of Life and Environment
and Earth Charter USA Campaign
Washington, DC, USA

F ollowing the 2002 United Nations' World Summit on
Sustainable Development, the Earth Charter Initiative
entered a new phase focused primarily on using the Earth
Charter as an educational tool and guide for local decision
making to create sustainable communities. Elizabeth Ferrero's and Joe Holland's book on the Earth Charter aids us all
in this task by helping us to reflect on the meaning of the
Earth Charter and how it can make a difference in our lives
and communities.

From August 26 to September 4, 2002, tens of thousands of
government and NGO delegates gathered in Johannesburg,
South Africa for the UN World Summit on Sustainable Development. This meeting took place on the 10th anniversary
of the 1992 UN Conference on Environment and Development (known popularly as the Earth Summit) held in Rio de
Janeiro, Brazil, and on the 30th anniversary of the 1972 UN
Conference on the Human Environment, held in Stockholm,
Sweden, and the first major UN meeting recognizing the importance of environmental issues. Also, during the past ten

19

years many more UN summits have been held – focusing on population, social development, women, cities, food, and other topics. Each has added more insight to our understanding of sustainable development.

Creating an Earth Charter was part of the unfinished business of the 1992 Rio Earth Summit. It had been originally called for by the UN World Commission on Environment and Development (also known as the Brundtland Commission), but was not achieved by the Rio process. In response, the Earth Council and Green Cross International, both devoted to the critical task of sustainable development, established the Earth Charter Initiative as a broad-based international mobilization for sustainable development.

As one among many significant social movements striving toward the emerging vision and sensibility of sustainable development, the Earth Charter has distinctive strengths to bring to the task of preparing society to embrace the new paradigm. Over the past decade, the Earth Charter movement has brought together tens of thousands of people representing hundreds of organizations to work in a participatory and transparent process to articulate the basic values and principles of sustainable development.

The Earth Charter document, developed within this process, represents a consensus vision of an integrated agenda for the pursuit of peace, social and economic justice, and the protection of biological diversity. It affirms that each of these important goals can only be achieved if all are achieved. Justice, peace, and ecological integrity are inextricably intertwined. We can only care for people if we care for the planet. We can only protect ecosystems if we care for people by providing freedom, eradicating poverty, and promoting good governance. The Earth Charter identifies, in a succinct and inspiring way, the necessary and sufficient conditions for promoting a just, peaceful, and sustainable future.

One goal of the Earth Charter Initiative has been to gain recognition of the Charter by the UN General Assembly. During past years major efforts have been made by Earth Charter Commissioners and the Earth Charter Secretariat to achieve this objective. The 2002 UN Summit in Johannesburg was an important step on the road toward reaching this long-term goal of recognition by the UN General Assembly.

The focus of the Johannesburg meeting was on developing a plan of practical action to implement the Rio Declaration, Agenda 21, and the goals of the UN Millennium Declaration – building on the commitments and recommendations of other major UN meetings held since Rio, including the Doha Development Declaration and the Monterrey Consensus. The major practical concerns were the eradication of poverty, overcoming the gulf between the rich and the poor, and reversing the trend of global environmental degradation.

At Johannesburg there was significant support for the Earth Charter by national governments. For example, in his address at the opening session of the World Summit, President Mbeki of South Africa cited the Earth Charter as a significant expression of "human solidarity" and as part of "the solid base from which the Johannesburg World Summit must proceed." Furthermore, in the closing days of the Summit, the first draft of the Political Declaration, known as the Johannesburg Declaration of Sustainable Development and prepared by South Africa, included in paragraph 13 recognition of "the relevance of the challenges posed in the Earth Charter." Unfortunately, on the last day of the Summit and in closed-door negotiations, the Declaration's reference to the Earth Charter was deleted. Even so, at the 2002 Summit the Earth Charter did receive much support. Additional heads of state, summit leaders, and major organizations spoke out for its importance.

Further, the Earth Charter Initiative developed a Type II partnership entitled "Educating for Sustainable Living with the Earth Charter," which was accepted by the Summit. Joining this partnership are the governments of Costa Rica, Honduras, Mexico, Niger, UNESCO, and thirteen NGOs. The goal of this initiative is to use the Earth Charter to provide education and training for local leaders and communities regarding the fundamental principles of sustainable development. A broader Earth Charter and Education program, developed by the Earth Charter Education Committee, provided a foundation for the creation of this partnership.

As substantial support for the Earth Charter continues to grow and as the document is used ever more widely as an educational tool and guide to action, the Earth Charter Initiative is becoming a significant global people's movement that can influence public policy and business practice as well as the choices and lifestyles of millions of individuals. Elizabeth and Joe's study book of reflection for action will be most useful in those tasks, and thus will contribute to our transition to a more ecologically sound, socially just, and peaceful future.

1

SPIRITUAL REGENERATION

AND THE

NEW PLANETARY CIVILIZATION

T he human journey has come to a major turning point. The materialistic and consumerist way of life that modern Western culture has so powerfully developed, and that is presently spreading across the entire planet, is not ecologically sustainable. That fact has been abundantly documented from a wide range of scientific sources. As a result, the human family, made up of so many diverse and creative cultures, is now called to seek a healing ecological path for our common planetary future.

Yet, like a dysfunctional family denying the presence of a destructive addiction in its midst, modern Western culture is still living in denial. Despite creative exceptions, so many modern institutions –business, government, education, relig-ion, and the arts – largely pretend that everything is OK. But everything is not OK.

Modern Western civilization is like a male racing-car driver speeding down a highway that ends in a cliff. Unaware that he is racing ever faster toward destruction, the driver rejoices in the machine that he controls and in the intelligence that designed it. From the partial viewpoint of the machine, it is indeed a great achievement. But from the holism of the surrounding geography, the driver is trapped in ignorance and foolhardiness. The faster the car goes, the sooner it and the driver will plunge over the cliff to their mutual destruction.

SPIRITUAL ROOTS OF THE ECOLOGICAL CRISIS

Some have argued that the deep roots of the modern ecological crisis of modern Western culture are to be found in greed. But that seems to be a superficial analysis, for there have been greedy people in every culture and at every time, yet only now do we face a foundational ecological crisis.

Others have argued that the roots of the modern ecological crisis are to be found in the Hebrew Scripture's Book of Genesis, with its theme of "domination" of Earth. But the ancient Hebrew peoples never produced great ecological destruction. In fact, the Hebrew Torah contains abundant legislation on how to care for Earth and all living things. Further, the Torah's narration of the covenant between the Children of Israel and the LORD portrays a three-way mutual relationship among the LORD, the people, and the land.

MODERN SPIRITUALITY & MECHANISTIC COSMOLOGY

We agree that the roots of the modern ecological crisis are spiritual, but we disagree that they are to be found in the ancient Book of Genesis. Rather, we propose, the spiritual roots of the modern ecological crisis arise from a distinctly modern form of cultural-spiritual consciousness.

In our view, the deepest root of the modern ecological crisis may be found in the unique cosmology that arose within the middle or bourgeois classes at the birth of the early modern Western world. This cosmology, which began in an early modern spirituality and philosophy, eventually expressed itself in modern science and supported an anti-ecological path for much of modern technology. We may describe this cosmology with its related paradigms of spirituality, philosophy, science, and technology as "mechanistic," meaning that it placed the image of a machine at the heart of its cosmological imagination.

The metaphor of the machine, at the root of the new modern cosmology, meant that over time the entire world would come to be perceived as a collection of autonomous parts (physical atoms, human individuals, academic disciplines, etc. – all unconnected to each other), In particular, the physical world of nature was seen as devoid of real life and spiritual meaning and to be understood only by reductionist methodologies. By contrast, earlier cosmologies from multiple cultures had seen the whole natural world as organic, that is, as holistic and alive, and also as bristling with spiritual presence.[1]

---

1   For a masterful study of the emergence of the modern mechanistic cosmology, with its loss of any sense of the sacred as mediated through nature, as well as of its hyper-masculine character and the significance of this loss for ecology, see Carolyn Merchant, THE DEATH OF NATURE: WOMEN, ECOLOGY, AND THE SCIENTIFIC REVOLUTION (San Francisco: Harper and Row, 1983). On the religious roots in medieval monastic culture of the modern, hyper-masculine, and mechanistic cosmology, see David Noble, A WORLD WITHOUT WOMEN: THE CHRISTIAN CLERICAL CULTURE OF

By constructing a mechanistic cosmology, modern bourgeois consciousness was cutting itself off culturally from spiritual nourishment by the Divine Energy sacramentally disclosed in and through Earth and the wider Cosmos. In this mechanistic cosmology, the natural world was seen only as a collection of disparate "resources" to be harnessed for utilitarian human purposes. Since the natural world was perceived as having no spiritual or ethical meaning of its own, then it could be plundered without limit and without concern for sustainability. The long-term result was, of course, the current ecological crisis, now being inflicted on the entire planet.

The mechanistic bourgeois cosmology took on initial strength with the European Christian Crusades against Islam. During this period, many merchants, traders, and craftspeople in European towns grew wealthy from the development of business related to war. The townspeople did not derive their livelihood from nature, as did the surrounding peasants who cultivated the land, but rather from mechanical production and related commerce. Hence they were not immersed in the spiritual energy of the natural world, but instead in the fabricated achievements of their workshops and stores.

The bourgeois cosmological vision gained greater strength with the rise of the European university system, aimed at serving especially the children of the expanding middle class. It also took powerful cultural expression with early modern philosophical and spiritual movements, known as the "*via*

WESTERN SCIENCE (New York: Alfred A. Knopf, 1992). On the birth of a fresh scientific cosmology that recovers the sense of the sacred in the natural world, see Rupert Sheldrake, THE REBIRTH OF NATURE: THE GREENING OF SCIENCE AND GOD (New York: Bantam Books, 1991).

moderna" and the "*devotio moderna*" (the "modern way" for philosophy and "modern devotionalism" for spirituality).

DENIAL OF SPIRITUAL PRESENCE
WITHIN THE NATURAL WORLD

Again, out of this bourgeois cosmological vision, modern science and technology arose, and they then produced the modern ecological crisis. But the modern forms of science and technology are not themselves the deep root of the problem. Rather it is the underlying mechanistic cosmology with its unique spirituality and philosophy that detach human meaning from the Divine Presence revealed in and through the spiritual energy of the natural world.

At the heart of the mechanistic cosmological vision, right from the beginning, was the claim that the Divine Mystery was not to be found in and through the natural world. To repeat, the modern bourgeois imagination saw the material world as devoid of spiritual meaning. In its view, spiritual meaning was totally transcendent, found only outside the world.

For this modern bourgeois mechanistic cosmology, the natural world was simply the great machine that God had created. God in turn was seen only as a great mechanical engineer, who had designed and fabricated the world, but then had left it to run on its own. God had made the natural world, the cosmology agreed; but, according to this view, God was no longer present in and through the natural world.

If this bourgeois cosmological vision found no Divine Presence in the natural world, then where did it find the Divine Presence? The bourgeois response was that the Divine Presence was to be found only in the inner recesses of the self, only in the emotional depth of the psyche. Exploration of the Divine Presence in the depth of the psyche was an important contribution of the *devotio moderna*. But rather than adding this psychological spirituality to the ancient nature spiritualities of the primal tribal religions and to the historical spiritualities of the classical Abrahamic spiritualities, the bourgeois understanding of God became only psychological. That was its deep flaw.

A strictly psychologized understanding of the divine Mystery would later express itself as religious privatization. Accepting religious privatization, one might appear to be profoundly religious in a psychological sense but become totally oblivious to the presence of the Divine Mystery in society, in history, and in the natural world.

Theorists of the modern European Enlightenment developed the early bourgeois mechanistic vision into a theory known as Deism. They argued that the Divine Mystery was a Divine clockmaker who designed a mechanical world, wound it up, and then let it run on its own with no spiritual meaning within creation itself. Still later major intellectual European movements of secularism and even aggressive atheism pushed the de-spiritualitization of the natural and socio-historical world even further, as they attempted to eliminate all public and educational references to spiritual meaning in nature, society, and history.

This modern bourgeois mechanistic vision stands in total opposition to the timeless wisdom of the most ancient spiritual traditions of Earth. From time immemorial, these ancient traditions, whose wisdom still continues in the native peoples and in the traditional peasantries, claimed to find God's presence profoundly revealed in the webs and cycles of nature.

For this reason, the ancient peoples approached the natural world with spiritual reverence and awe; and they based their spiritual rituals largely on the webs and cycles of the natural world.

By contrast, as we have seen, the modern bourgeois denial of any spiritual meaning within the natural world meant that the natural world suddenly became available for limitless economic plunder. For economic plunder was now under no spiritual restraint. The result of limitless plunder of the natural world, and of technological attempts to treat the natural world as if it were itself a machine, is the present ecological crisis.

The Earth Charter calls us to a path beyond the mechanistic cosmology of late modern Western culture. It calls us to embrace a new cosmology which recalls that we are part of Earth, and that what we do to Earth we do to ourselves. Further, the Earth Charter spells out in multiple principles what it means to care for Earth in a truly sustainable way.

THE NEED FOR A NEW PLANETARY CIVILIZATION

The Earth Charter emerges against the threatening horizon of powerful economic forces attempting to draw all the peoples of Earth into the way of life of the modern Western middle classes, that is, into a materialistic civilization of endless consumerism.

It seems dubious that this project will succeed, since so many people across the planet are becoming marginalized from the land and cast as an impoverished underclass into poverty-filled mega-cities. Even worse, the more that people across Earth embrace the materialist and consumerist way of life of the Western middle classes, the more rapid the triumph of a now globalized mechanistic civilization that is ecologically unsustainable.

Gratefully the Earth Charter issues a powerful call arising from all the peoples of Earth to seek a different ethical vision, one that is ecologically sustainable. This ethical call of the Earth Charter needs to become, we propose, a key foundation for a new planetary civilization. In the "dialogue among civilizations" currently underway across the world, the perspective of ecological ethics needs to become foundational.

THE NEED TO RECOVER
A COSMOLOGICAL SPIRITUALITY

We rejoice that the Earth Charter calls all people of Earth to an ethics of ecology. We ourselves have dedicated our efforts in this small book to help people understand better this call of the Earth Charter. But for the call of the Earth Charter to bear abundant fruit, we propose that there needs also to be a profound recovery of spiritual meaning mediated in and through the natural world.

The Earth Charter speaks ethically of Earth as a "sacred trust." We affirm that ethical way of speaking of Earth, but we also suggest going beyond that formulation to speak spiritually of Earth itself as revealing the sacred. Seeing Earth as revealing the sacred will enable us to return in a healing way to celebrate the most ancient source of spirituality for human consciousness, that is, the mystical and presence of the Divine Mystery in the depths of all creation.

Along with the ancient primal religions still found in all the cultures of all regions of Earth, the three great classical religions of Judaism, Christianity, and Islam also saw creation as revealing the sacred. These three Abrahamic religions all affirm the statement of the book of Genesis that creation is an expression of the word of God, and as such reveals a Divine communication. Thus, Genesis 1:3 proclaims, "God said 'Let there be light,' and so there was light." According to Genesis, the light is the continuing expression of the creative word of God. So too, the land, the sky, the sun, the moon, the flowers, the birds, the animals, the fish, and all of creation communicate the loving presence of the Divine Mystery.

Recovering this wise consciousness from ancient peoples and from the classical Abrahamic religions (awareness that the created world is bristling with the communication of the Divine Mystery) is, we believe, the foundational step toward making real the ethical vision of the Earth Charter. This possibility is even more enhanced by the dawning consciousness of evolution as an artistic process, rooted in turn in Divine Creativity.

We conclude here with the lyrical words of Thomas Berry, which capture so well this need to regenerate a cosmological spiritual vision, now enhanced by the discovery of evolution:

> *Central to this process is our contact with the sacred*
> *and the vast range of Earth's psychic dynamics. While*
> *our sense of the sacred can never be recovered precisely as*
> *it existed in former centuries, it can be recovered in the*
> *mystique of Earth, in the epic of evolution. Spiritual*
> *disciplines are once again being renewed throughout the*
> *world . . . We must feel that we are supported by that*
> *same power that brought Earth into being, that power*

that spun the galaxies into space, that lit the sun and brought the moon into its orbit. . . We are ourselves a mystical quality of Earth.[2]

2   Thomas Berry, THE GREAT WORK: OUR WAY INTO THE FUTURE (New York: Bell Tower, 1999), pp. 174-175.

2

UNITED NATIONS STEPS

TOWARD THE EARTH CHARTER

T he Earth Charter is essentially a people's treaty. Therefore the final version of the Earth Charter is the prod-
uct of a decade of consultation around the globe. People
with different social, economic and ethnic backgrounds dia-
logued together with the aim of developing an international
document that would transcend their differences and establish common principles as guidelines for the future of humankind.

On March 24, 2000, the Earth Charter Commission issued a
final version of the document. (See the full text in an Appendix.) However, since the Earth Charter is a vibrant document empowering the lives of the peoples of Earth, the
Commission has reserved the right to make additional ad-
justments to the wording of the Earth Charter, if dictated by
real needs of the people of Earth.

The Commission's plan is to take the Earth Charter to the
United Nations for endorsement as the fulfillment of something begun at the Rio Earth Summit. With the endorsement
of the UN, the Earth Charter will become a "soft law"
document, whose principles are not binding; however, inter-

national law has proven that soft law tends to become "hard law" with the passing of time.[1]

In the Earth Charter, for the first time in human history, environmental rights are not perceived as another aspect of human rights, which would represent a utilitarian perspective of the natural world. The Earth Charter recognizes that the natural world has intrinsic value in itself. Yet the language used does not expound an anti-humanistic philosophy of eco-centrism; rather humans are perceived as stewards of the natural world. In addition, the central theme of the Earth Charter is the relationship of humans to nature. Thus, interdependence is affirmed in all its principles.[2] The Earth Charter calls for a just and sustainable way of life, where the human and the non-human live systemically in a symbiotic relationship.

Moreover specifically human socio-economic issues are at the core of most of the Earth Charter Principles. In its conclusion titled "The Way Forward," the Earth Charter also calls for personal transformation, so that both the socio-economic order of today and our relationship to the natural world can truly change.[3]

---

1   Steven Rockefeller, "An Introduction to the Text of the Earth Charter," a paper presented at an on-line Academic Conference entitled GLOBAL ETHICS: SUSTAINABLE DEVELOPMENT AND THE EARTH CHARTER, April 1999 at www.earthcharter.org/files/resources/ef_rockefeller.htm.

2   Mary Evelyn Tucker, "Reflections on the Earth Charter," a paper presented at the April 1999 on-line Academic Conference entitled GLOBAL ETHICS: SUSTAINABLE DEVELOPMENT AND THE EARTH CHARTER. at www.earthcharter.org/files/resources/ef_tucker.htm.

3   THE EARTH CHARTER, Final Version, p. 6.

As we will see later, the Earth Charter heralds a new global ethic, grounded in two fundamental principles: *sustainable development* and *environmental conservation.*

Of great significance in drafting the Earth Charter have been multiple United Nations conferences, plus the many declarations and treaties pertaining to environment and sustainable development as well as the many declarations and "people's treaties" developed by non-governmental agencies. The many voices from civic society, especially in the last decade, have been a determining factor in giving more space in the Earth Charter to women, the poor, and the indigenous people all around the globe on how environmental degradation and lack of sustainable development have kept them in bondage.

Before addressing the Charter itself, let us briefly examine earlier United Nations documents leading up to the Earth Charter Initiative.

1972 - THE STOCKHOLM DECLARATION

Ecology was not a main concern of the United Nations when it was founded in 1945. After World War II, international security, human rights, and economic development became the most urgent issues. In the 1970s, however, people's attentions started to turn to the devastation of the environment being caused by pollution. Moreover there was developing an increasingly influential global civil society, especially with the new technologies linking the people of Earth. Non-governmental agencies started to play an increasingly important role -- drafting and circulating all types of declarations and "people's treaties" to protect the natural world, the indigenous people of Earth, the poor, and women, while heralding a sustainable way of life.

Because of these developments, the United Nations called for a conference on the environment. It was planned for Stockholm from 5 to 16 June 1972, under the leadership of the Canadian Maurice Strong. As the Stockholm conference's final declaration made clear, its purpose was "to inspire and guide the peoples of the world in the preservation and enhancement of the human environment."[4] The result was the *Declaration of the United Nations Conference on the Human Environment,* actually consisting of 6 declarations and 26 principles and organized around four major points:

1. The right to all people to a healthy environment;
2. Intergenerational integrity;
3. Assistance to developing countries; and
4. Protection from pollution.

The focus of the Stockholm Conference, however, was solely on industrial pollution of air and water. Concern for developing countries was exclusively around problems caused by such industrial pollution. Further, the terminology used was not inclusive of gender -- with constant use throughout the document of the term "man" instead of "human." The document also clearly revealed a lack of awareness of the deeper ecological and social problems that we humans face at the end of the industrial era. In summary, the Stockholm Declaration remained within the boundaries of human-rights language.

One major point to note is that out of the principles generated by this Human Environment Conference came the

---

4   DECLARATION OF THE UNITED NATIONS CONFERENCE ON THE HUMAN ENVIRONMENT (Nairobi: United Nations Environmental Program, 1972), Part I, par. 3. The text may be found on the Internet at the UNEP's website, www.unep.org.

founding of the United Nations Environment Program (UNEP). The UNEP represents the environmental conscience of the United Nations system.[5]

After the Earth Summit in Rio de Janeiro, Brazil (1992), the UNEP was challenged to integrate with its environmental objectives the concept of sustainable development. Finally, in 1997, from its headquarters in Nairobi, Kenya, the UNEP responded with the Nairobi Declaration. In this document, the UNEP declared its role as promoting a greater awareness about the environment and as bringing about greater cooperation (par. 3.e.). Also, it stressed the importance of working more at the local level to promote regional endeavors (par. 3.a.) Overall in the years since Rio, the UNEP has worked diligently to make information available about and to facilitate training programs in sustainability, especially through its regional offices that work with local governments and non-governmental organizations to solve the problems of specific local communities.[6]

1982 - THE WORLD CHARTER FOR NATURE

In 1982, the General Assembly of the United Nations adopted the World Charter for Nature. This important document is in many ways the true precursor of the Earth Charter. Its publication marked the first time that respect of

---

5   For general information on the UNEP, see its Internet website at www.unep.org.

6   The UNEP has regional offices for Africa; Latin America and the Caribbean; West Asia; Asia and the Pacific; Europe; and North America. Again, for the text of the Nairobi Declaration and other UNEP materials, see its Internet website at www.unep.org.

the natural world was officially perceived as the main reason for protecting the environment.[7]

The World Charter for Nature emphasized the universal responsibility of all peoples to safeguard resources for future generations and to protect and restore the natural world. By contrast, the Stockholm Declaration had clearly listed only the economic and social concerns of humans. In the World Charter for Nature, authentic ecological concerns appeared for the first time. This was a major breakthrough.

There was also an initial attempt made in the World Charter for Nature to use an integrated approach linking socio-economic concerns with ecological ones. Unfortunately this occurred only in the Preamble. In the body of the document, the issue of poverty did not receive the attention that it deserved, plus there was no mention of women, youth, or indigenous people. Thus we would have to wait for the Earth Charter for a more consistent and comprehensive approach that seeks to conserve, improve and expand together our integrated ecological and human well-being.

Also the World Charter for Nature still used the sexist term "mankind" instead of the more inclusive term "humankind." In addition, in the World Charter for Nature, "nature" refers to the non-human dimension, with no holistic understanding that we humans are also part of nature."[8]

---

7   WORLD CHARTER FOR NATURE (New York: United Nations, 1982), available on the United Nations Internet website at www.un.org/documents/ga/res/37/a37r007.htm.

8   Thomas Berry's concept of humans and the natural world as one entity is at the heart of the Earth Charter. In the World Charter for Nature, however, humans and nature are seen as two separate entities. For Berry's perspective, see THE DREAM OF EARTH (San Francisco, CA: Sierra Club Books, 1988).

Lastly, in contrast to today's consciousness, the concept of optimum sustainable development was not included in the World Charter for Nature. The document did note, however, the impact of unsustainable consumption and production, and it asserted the right of public participation. The main drawback here, however, was the lack of any reference to the ethical responsibility of *care* for all forms of life --- and also there was no spiritual vision that went beyond the Kantian ethical principle of *duty*. In the Earth Charter we will find the concept of sacred *trust* that humans feel and have towards the natural world -- in a true spirit of stewardship.

1987 - THE BRUNDTLAND REPORT

The World Commission on Environment and Development (WCED) was established as a result of the United National General Assembly's 38th session meeting in 1983. The UN's Secretary-General appointed as Chairperson Ms. Gro Harlem Brundtland of Norway, formerly Prime Minister of that country and currently leader of the Norwegian Labor Party, and Dr. Mansour Khalid, the former Minister of Foreign Affairs of Sudan, as Vice-Chairperson.

After several years of work, the World Commission on Environment and Development, which met at Stockholm in 1987, presented its report, Our Common Future, to the UN General Assembly. Sustainable development and environmental protection were central issues, and these would later become the two key themes of the Earth Charter. Because Dr. Brundtland chaired the Commission, its final document is often referred to as the Brundtland Report.

The Commission declared that environment and development are inseparable. Furthermore, it added that in order for both to be in harmony, development must be "sustainable," i.e., "nature must be used on a basis that can be sustained into the distant future."[9]

Early on the concept of "sustainable development" had been used in the World Conservation Strategy formulated in 1980 by the International Union for the Conservation of Nature (IUCN) in cooperation with the United Nations Environmental Program (UNEP) and the World Wildlife Fund (WWF). The Strategy recognized that "the planet's capacity to support people is being undermined by poor land management, profligate use of resources, and the sort of grinding poverty that forces people to destroy the very resources they need to survive."[10]

The novelty of the 1987 report was in further defining "sustainable development" and understanding that for an economy to be sustainable, many issues must be looked at: for example, population growth, urbanization, poverty, human health, the environment, and quality of life.

The Brundtland Report, Our Common Future, also recommended the creation of a "new charter." The report stated: "the charter should prescribe new norms for state and interstate behavior needed to maintain livelihood and life on our

---

9   United Nations Association of Canada, ON THE ROAD TO BRAZIL, Series
     Issue Paper, No. 1 (Edmonton, Alberta: UNAC, 1991), p. 1.

10   See the prior reference, p. 2, and also IUCN, UNEP, and WFF, WORLD
     CONSERVATION STRATEGY: LIVING RESOURCE CONSERVATION FOR
     SUSTAINABLE DEVELOPMENT (Gland: International Union for Conservation
     of Nature and Natural Resources, 1980).

shared planet."[11] The charter was to deal with the increasingly international economic reality of developed and developing countries. The report called for urgent economic reforms, in order for long-term "sustainable growth" to become an effective tool for changes in lifestyles. In addition, it stated, more opportunities for trade and economic growth were needed for developing countries to become self-reliant.[12]

1992 - THE RIO DECLARATION

The final and major UN influence on the development of the Earth Charter came from the Conference on Environment and Development (UNCED), held 3-14 June 1992 in Rio de Janeiro, Brazil. This meeting took place on the 20th anniversary of the 1972 UN Conference on the Human Environment held in Stockholm. The UNCED's Secretary-General was Maurice F. Strong of Canada; and Tommy Koh of Singapore chaired the event.

This important gathering had been prepared for two years by discussions and negotiations among more than 100 nations. The actual UNCED Rio gathering, again popularly called the "the Earth Summit," brought together delegates from more than 150 nations, activists from some 1,400 non-governmental organizations (NGOs), approximately 8,000 journal-

---

11   Our Common Future, p. 332.

12   Our Common Future, Annex 1, "Summary of Proposed Legal Principles for Environmental Protection and Sustainable Development by the WCED Experts Group on Environmental Law, p. 2.

ists, and thousands of Brazilians.[13] The focus of UNCED was, as its name stated, *environment and development*, and the ramifications were broad and varied.

At the meeting, there was a sense of urgency about the need to draft an "Earth Charter" that would include awareness of the increasing disparity between the developed people of the North and the developing countries of the South in their distinct responses to environmental degradation and economic development. In Rio, various non-governmental organizations (NGOs) prepared and circulated several drafts, but no formal United Nations "the Earth Charter" was ever accepted. The Rio Declaration on Environment and Development became the only document officially issued by the meeting.

As a result of the UNCED meeting, a new United Nations body was established, the Sustainable Development Commission. Further, two new international institutions were inspired by the event: the World Business Council for Sustainable Development; and the Earth Council. The Earth Council, led by Maurice Strong and including a committee of 28 internationally known scientists, was established in Costa Rica immediately following the event. The Earth Charter Initiative and the Earth Charter Commission would come out of the Planet the Earth Council.[14]

---

13 Peter Haas, Marc Levy, and Edward Parson, "Appraising the Earth Summit; How should we judge UNCED's success?," ENVIRONMENT 30 (8): 6-11, 26-33.

14 Information on the United Nations Sustainable Development Commission may be found at www.un.org/esa/sustdev; on the World Business Council for Sustainable Development at www.wbcsd.ch; and on the Earth Council website at www.ecouncil.ac.cr.

The Rio Declaration, like earlier UN documents, still had many shortcomings. First of all, it remained anthropocentric by still seeing humans as not within nature. Also, the document did mention the concept of precaution, but it said nothing about prevention. Also gender played no vital role in its framework of reference. In addition, the text remained imprisoned within the perimeters of national boundaries.

Further, the Rio Declaration showed no awareness of an evolving universe and no understanding of the common burden we carry of stewardship for intergenerational equity. Moreover, the document contained no concept of environmental justice, and it failed to base global environmental ethics on the sacred trust of human responsibility for Earth. The language used showed *respect* towards the natural world, but it lacked a sense of *reverence* – something that the Earth Charter would make central.

The most recent UN conference on Ecology was the World Summit on Sustainable Development (WSSD), which met from 26 August to 4 September 2002 in Johannesburg, South Africa. While this meeting remains a significant event in the history of growing ecological consciousness across the UN system, it proved somewhat disappointing for many ecologists because it failed to adopt specific deadlines and benchmarks for achieving certain ecological goals, for example, in the use of renewable energy sources.

In a similar vein, as Richard M. Clugston has pointed out in his Forward to this book, the WSSD provided both gains and disappointments for Earth Charter advocates. A full report on the WSSD in relation to the Earth Charter, "The Earth Charter at the Johannesburg Summit: A Report Prepared by the Earth Charter Steering Committee and International Secretariat" (November 2002), has been prepared by the Earth Charter Steering Committee and International Secretariat and is available at the Earth Charter website (www.earthcharter.org).

On the negative side, according to the Report, the WSSD did not formally endorse the Earth Charter, something which had been recommended by Secretary General Kofi Annan's High Level Advisory Panel for the meeting, and which Maurice Strong had publicly promoted at a June 2002 gathering in Rio de Janeiro. Further, it even dropped a reference to the Earth Charter that had been included in the first draft of the Johannesburg Declaration.

On the positive side, again according to the Report, the Earth Charter cause was significantly advanced at the Summit. Central ideas from the Earth Charter were to found in the Johannesburg Declaration, and a significant number of governments and non-governmental organizations supported the Earth Charter. Most importantly, the Summit endorsed an official "Type II" educational partnership with the Earth Charter Initiative titled "Educating for Sustainable Living" and oriented toward "education and training for local leaders and communities." In addition, the Earth Charter Education Committee prepared a whole "Earth Charter and Education program." Similarly, the United Nations specialized agency for education, science, and culture, UNESCO, established two additional educational partnerships, one titled "Global Higher Education for Sustainability" and the other "Teaching and Learning for a Sustainable Future."

Thus we have seen that from 1972 to the present, there has been an evolving and expanding consciousness of ecology in the UN system and among NGOs from around the world.

Each of the UN documents has made an important contribution, but each still fell short in certain areas.

CHART 1 – CHRONOLOGY OF DOCUMENTS

DATE	DOCUMENT	UNITED NATIONS
1972	STOCKHOLM DECLARATION	UN CONFERENCE ON THE HUMAN ENVIRONMENT
1982	WORLD CHARTER FOR NATURE	UN GENERAL ASSEMBLY
1987	BRUNDTLAND REPORT	UN WORLD COMMISSION ON ENVIRONMENT AND DEVELOPMENT
1992	RIO DECLARATION	UN CONFERENCE ON ENVIRONMENT AND DEVELOPMENT
2002	JOHANNESBURG DECLARATION	UN WORLD SUMMIT ON SUSTAINABLE DEVELOPMENT

Having reviewed these United Nations activities in relationship to the Earth Charter, let us now turn to examine the Earth Charter Initiative, which, as we will see, goes beyond the limitations of these UN documents.

3

THE INTERNATIONAL

EARTH CHARTER INITIATIVE

O ne of the most important outcomes of the Rio the
Earth Summit was the creation of the Earth Council,
noted at the end of the last chapter. Once established, the
Council had as its goal pursuit of the unfinished business of
the Earth Summit. Top among its priorities for this goal was
the creation of an Earth Charter document that would arise
from the peoples of Earth and could be accepted by the
United Nations.

THE LEADERSHIP

In 1994, Maurice Strong, Chairman of the newly formed
Earth Council and the former Secretary-General of both the
Stockholm Conference and the UNCED meeting, joined
together with Mikhail Gorbachev, former Premier of the now
dissolved Soviet Union and President of the ecologically oriented body that he founded, Green Cross International. Together the two figures launched the Earth Charter Initiative,
the movement charged with drafting the document. Jim

MacNeil, former secretary of World Commission on Environment and Development, and Ruud Lubbers, Prime Minister of the Netherlands, facilitated the project, while Ambassador Mohamed Sahnoun of Algeria served as the project's Executive Director during its first phase.[1]

THE FIRST CONSULTATION

In 1995 and 1996, the Earth Charter Initiative focused on gathering background data and documents that would be useful for establishing a set of values and principles to incorporate into the Charter. A major study and a detailed commentary on over 50 international law documents was presented to the first international conference, which met in May of 1995 at The Hague.[2] Representatives from over thirty countries and seventy organizations participated in the conference.[3] Out of the conference two Main Principles emerged:

- Environmental Conservation;
- Sustainable Development.

The conference demonstrated increased awareness by its participants that humanity needed a set of guidelines that would unite all the peoples of the globe in a common spiri-

---

1   THE EARTH CHARTER INITIATIVE HANDBOOK (San José, Costa Rica: the Earth Charter Initiative Secretariat, no date), p. 25 at www.earthcharter.org/files/resources/ACF1C89.pdf

2   Steven Rockefeller, PRINCIPLES OF ENVIRONMENTAL CONSERVATION AND SUSTAINABLE DEVELOPMENT: SUMMARY AND SURVEY (San José, Costa Rica: the Earth Charter INitiative Secretariat, 1996).

3   THE EARTH CHARTER INITIATIVE HANDBOOK, p. 31.

tual vision reverencing all forms of creation — in language that would be clear and simple -- and would echo the dreams and aspiration of all humanity across present and future generations.

In 1997, the Earth Charter Initiative decided to establish an organization to support the process that would bring to fruition the Earth Charter document. Together with Green Cross International, the Earth Charter Initiative formed the Earth Charter Commission.

Eventually appointed at various times to the Commission were the following members, including 5 co-chairs, with all selected to represent the peoples of the globe. The members were:

FOR AFRICA AND THE MIDDLE EAST

- Amadou Toumani Touré, Mali (co-chair)
- Princess Basma Bint Talal, Jordan
- Wangari Maathai, Kenya
- Mohamed Sahnoun, Algeria

FOR ASIA AND THE PACIFIC

- Kamla Chowdhry, India (co-chair)
- A.T. Ariyarante, Sri Lanka
- Wakako Hironaka, Japan
- Pauline Tangiora, New Zealand/Aoteroa
- Erna Witoelar, Indonesia

FOR EUROPE

- Mikhail Gorbachev, Russia (Co-Chair)
- Pierre Calame, France

- Ruud F. M. Lubbers, The Netherlands
- Federico Mayor, Spain
- Henriette Rasmussen, Artic/Greenland (Inuit)
- Awaraham Soetendorp, The Netherlands

FOR LATIN AMERICA AND THE CARIBBEAN

- Mercedes Sosa, Argentina (Co-Chair)
- Leonardo Boff, Brazil
- Yolanda Kakabadse, Ecuador
- Shridath Ramphal, Guyana

FOR NORTH AMERICA

- Maurice F. Strong, Canada (Co-chair)
- John Hoyt, United States of America
- Elizabeth May, Canada
- Steven Rockefeller, United States of America
- Severn Cullis-Suzuki, Canada

The Commission's main task was to oversee the consultation and drafting process of the document, which would be called the "Earth Charter," and to approve its final version.

STEERING COMMITTEE AND SECRETARIAT

The Commission also established two other bodies:

- The Earth Charter Steering Committee;
- The Earth Charter International Secretariat.

The Steering Committee was chaired by the members of the Commission and entrusted with overseeing the operations and programs of the Earth Charter.

The Secretariat was established at the Earth Council headquarters, eventually located in Costa Rica on the campus of the University for Peace in San José. Maximo Kalaw of the Philippines was originally appointed Executive Director, and a small body of staff and volunteers provided the needed support for the Commission and for the Steering Committee. The Executive Director is Marian Vilela, and the body's office is at the following address:

The Earth Charter International Campaign Secretariat
c/o The Earth Council
PO Box 319-6100, San José, Costa Rica
Phone: (506) 205-3500 ; Fax: (506) 249-3500
Email : info@earthcharter.org
Website: www.earthcharter.org

NATIONAL COMMITTEES

An important aspect of the Earth Charter Initiative has been to make sure that the Earth Charter would be a "people's treaty" — becoming part of the local reality and empowering local inhabitants around the globe. In order to accomplish this goal, the Commission called for National Committees to be established in various countries of the world. At the present moment, there are 53 Earth Charter National Committees.[4]

The Earth Charter National Committees are formed by representatives from local business, religious groups, women's groups, educational bodies, and other organizations of civil society. During the years of the Consultation process these committees discussed and took ownership of the various drafts of the Earth Charter. They sent back to the Commis-

---

4   THE EARTH CHARTER INITIATIVE HANDBOOK, p. 8.

sion their input concerning the wording and values that the various drafts incorporated. In some countries, National Councils of Sustainable Development (NCSDs) served as the Earth Charter National Committees. The Secretariat in Costa Rica oversaw and worked closely with the National Committees and the National Councils on Sustainable Development.

The main job of each National Committee has been to take the Earth Charter to the people of their own country or city, and to let the people interpret the document for themselves in order to take ownership of its values and ideas. This "bottom-up" strategy has proven successful and has manifested different and creative efforts all around the globe. In some countries, like the United States and Canada, resources and technology have allowed the process to make very significant changes in the lives of the people. In other countries, the purpose of the National Committees has been to simply introduce the Earth Charter to the local people and explain its principle. Every sector of civil society from law to business has been actively engaged with the Earth Charter.

The main impetus was during 1999 when most National Committees emerged, especially in Africa, Asia and the Pacific.[5] Education has been one of the main areas in which Australia has disseminated the Earth Charter. The Australian Earth Charter Steering Committee has successfully brought together a large sector of civil society with educators to dialogue and plan activities. They have developed significant

---

5   An excellent resource for a detailed account of the activities of the National Committees of the Earth Charter during the years 1999 and 2000 is the Earth Charter STATUS REPORT 1999/2000 (San José, Costa Rica: the Earth Charter International Campaign Secretariat, 2000). This and other resources may be found at the official web site of the Earth Charter at www.earthcharter.org.

curriculum material relating to the Earth Charter for their school system. Moreover, different regional Earth Charter Committees have been established in various parts of the country: in Queensland, Victoria, South Australia, Western Australia and Tasmania.

For the rest of Asia and the Pacific, there have been activities in Hong Kong, with a Sustainable Development Forum, and with research on the Earth Charter done by the City University of Hong Kong. In India, the Environment Education Council for Children of the Delhi Public School System held an evening of Christian, Vedic and Muslim hymns as offerings to Earth. Moreover, a document called "Soul Force for Sustainability" has been produced in order to encourage sustainability.

In Europe, new National Committees have been formed in Austria, France, Italy and Norway. The focus in Europe has been the dissemination and translation of the Earth Charter in the schools, businesses and local non-governmental organizations.

Latin America has been quite active with the Earth Charter process, especially in Brazil, Colombia, and Costa Rica. A wide variety of activities have taken place. Children from the primary and secondary schools in Costa Rica have played a significant role in taking ownership of the Earth Charter principles by applying it to their own reality.

In the United States a large Earth Charter USA Campaign was established to develop activities and to provide information and resources to help people in all sectors of society embrace the values and ideas of the Earth Charter. Moreover, the Earth Charter Working Groups were organized to address the many issues present in the Charter, particularly those relevant to business and labor, government, communications, education, and so forth.

Besides the National Committees, there were all over the globe in 1999 multiple conferences and various activities sponsored by non-governmental organizations embracing the values and principles of the Earth Charter. Examples include the Indigenous People's Campaign; the Paulo Freire Institute initiative to introduce the Charter in the educational system; and the World Council of Churches' significant discussions for two and half days on how to promote the Charter in their congregations.[6]

During 1999 the work of the National Committees was primarily to establish themselves and to a great extent to study the principles of the Charter. They did this first of all by translating the document into their own languages and then discussing it among themselves. Then starting with the year 2000, National Committees endorsed the Earth Charter's principles of sustainable development and environmental protection by using those ideas in their personal lives and in the organizations to which they belong.

In the Spring of 2000, the Russian Association of the Indigenous People of the North (RAIPON) formally endorsed the Earth Charter. The Millennium NGO Forum in May brought together more than 1,000 non-governmental agencies for its meeting at the United Nations in New York and formally endorsed the Earth Charter in its final report and declaration. In June, both Green Cross International and the Sierra Club of Canada endorsed the Charter as well and recommended that its members apply its principles to their lives. In July,

---

6   THE EARTH CHARTER STATUS REPORT 1999/2000, p. 51.

endorsement came from the Third Special Assembly of the Amazonian Parliament, held in Lima, Peru, as well as in November from the Council of the University for Peace in Costa Rica.

Of great significance were the dialogues that the Earth Charter has fostered in over 40 countries of the globe. The Charter has been used and continues to be used in local community groups as the foundation of a new global ethic. Its principles have been incorporated in workshops, roundtable discussions, school curricula, and conferences to motivate people and to foster their dreams. Most importantly, thanks to the document, the natural world has become part of many celebratory rites and thus has powerfully affected many people's spirituality.

The process continues. At the present time there are over 50 national committees worldwide. In February 2001, the National Wildlife Federation of the US, with a membership of over 4 million people, endorsed the Earth Charter. Now, with a final version of the Earth Charter in place, the Earth Charter Commission has set up an International Steering Committee for the implementation of major Earth-Charter activities around the world.

On June 8, 2001 in Urbino, Italy, the Earth Charter was formally presented by Mikhail Gorbachev, President of Green Cross International. The event was sponsored by Italy's President, Carlo Azeglio Ciampi, and was attended by international leading names in all areas of civic society. Urbino, the first Renaissance city, is the symbol of a sustainable way of life and has set the tone for future activities.

On September 29, 2001, there were Earth Charter Community Summits held in 12 cities of the United States, and in

2002 the list expanded to 24 cities. These grass-roots summits, extended in 2001 by satellite communications, helped each community to take ownership of the Charter by planning activities developed over the year, and then to uplink with each other and dialogue at the close.[7]

In addition, from November 28 through December 2, 2001, the "2001 Asia Pacific the Earth Charter Conference" met in Brisbane, Australia to provide practical examples and assistance to implement the Earth Charter in government, business and the environment across the Asia Pacific Region.

COOPERATING ORGANIZATIONS

Lastly, there are several pre-existing organizations that have made a long-term commitment to work with the Earth Charter Initiative. Cooperating with the Earth Charter Secretariat, these bodies are:

- The Earth Council;
- Green Cross International;
- The Foundation for the Survival and Development of Humanity;
- The Center for Respect of Life and Environment;
- The Center for Dignity and Rights/Cedar International;
- The International Council for Local Environmental Initiatives;
- The Paulo Freire Institute;
- The Association of University Leaders for a Sustainable Future;

---

7   For more information, see the Earth Charter Community Summits website at www.earthchartersummits.org.

- Global Education Associates;
- The Inuit Circumpolar Conference.

Another important part of the Earth Charter Initiative was the creation of an International Drafting Committee, headed by Steven Rockefeller, Professor of Religion at Middlebury College, Vermont, USA. This Committee had as its main task the actual writing of the various the Earth Charter drafts and then the production of its final version. The members of the drafting committee were:

- Steven Rockefeller, United States (Chairperson)
- Johannah Bernstein, Canada
- Adelardo Brenes, Costa Rica
- J. Ronald Engel, United States
- Brendan Mackey, Australia
- Paul Raskin, United States
- Mirian Vilela, Brazil
- Christine von Weizsäcker, Germany

Moreover, many others attended various meetings and participated in the drafting process of the Earth Charter.

In March 1997, the "Rio+5 Forum" met in Rio de Janeiro, Brazil. The Earth Council organized this Forum, and brought together from the peoples of the globe over 500 representatives of non-governmental organizations (NGOs) and National Councils on Sustainable Development (NCSDs).[8] A Benchmark Draft of the Earth Charter became the focal point of the six-day consultation.

---

8   THE Earth Charter INITIATIVE HANDBOOK, p. 29.

The Benchmark Draft contained a short preamble, plus 18 principles and a conclusion. The document began with the following statement that signaled the new historical moment:

> *At this unprecedented time of opportunity and danger, when life on Earth is being placed at risk, it is imperative that we, the People of Earth, declare our interdependence with and responsibilities with each other, the larger community of life, and the evolving universe. In the midst of a magnificent diversity of cultures and life forms, we are one humanity and one Earth community with a common future.*[9]

After Rio+5, the Earth Charter consultation gained momentum. Conferences, meetings, and dialogues proliferated across the globe. People studied the Earth Charter Benchmark Draft in schools and businesses, as well as in the homes and religious centers of thousands and thousands of people. The Earth Council also established an Earth Charter Internet web site at www.earthcharter.org.

During 1997 and 1998, the Earth Charter National Committees formed in 35 different countries, from North America to Africa, Asia, and Europe. For the first time in its history, the Earth Charter started to become a familiar name. The Benchmark Draft was translated into multiple languages. Children began to use the Draft in their classrooms. Businesses saw the Draft as an opportune moment to fund and sponsor activities based on its principles. National Regional Committees used the Draft's values according to the needs of their local communities. In sum, creative, diverse, and energetic projects exploded across the planet.

---

9   BENCHMARK DRAFT II, Paragraph 1.

With the creative energies of the work of the National Committees came the need to look at the Benchmark Draft text itself, and to decide if and how it met the needs, values, and dreams of the people of Earth. In early 1999 a drafting international meeting was held in New York City to incorporate the input of the National Committees and various other organizations into a new draft of the Earth Charter.[10] Representatives came from Argentina, Australia, Brazil, Canada, Costa Rica, Germany, Kenya, India, the Netherlands, the Philippines, Pakistan, Russia, and the United States.[11]

In April of 1999, Benchmark Draft II was born. The new draft contained some major changes. First of all, the language of the Charter became more inclusive of the varied people of Earth. Second, the Main Principles were reduced to 16, with 65 Supporting Principles. Thanks to the consultation process organized by various National Committees, Benchmark Draft II spread all over the globe. In 1999, there also appeared translations of the Earth Charter in many of the 35 countries where the text had been circulating.

The Earth Charter Secretariat also organized two academic on-line conferences, one in English in April 1999, and another in Spanish in November of the same year. The English

---

10   The meeting was held at the Pocantico Conference Center of the Rockefeller Brothers Fund.

11   The on-line Conference in English, in April 1999, with 17 invited speakers, had video-presentations and on-line discussions. More than 300 universities in 76 countries participated. The on-line Conference in Spanish held in November of the same year, had more than 350 students in 25 countries who participated to the 12 presentations. THE EARTH CHARTER INITIATIVE HANDBOOK, p. 27.

on-line conference was conducted over a two-week period and attracted people from 76 countries and 300 universities.[12]

The momentum of the Earth Charter consultation reached its peak in 1999 with myriad national conferences, symposia, round-table discussions, and projects of various sorts discussing the principles of the Earth Charter and how they applied to their own local reality. Moreover the number of National Committees grew to over 45. In October 1999, many of these representatives participated in a ten-day on-line conference that focused on the text of the document.[13] The goal of the Earth Charter to become a people's treaty now became a reality.

2000 - THE FINAL VERSION

In January and February 2000 the drafting committee worked intensively to finalize the Earth Charter. In mid-March at UNESCO headquarters in Paris, the Earth Charter Commission completed its final changes. On 24 March, the committee released the final version of the Earth Charter. But the Commission reserved the right within the next five years to make additional changes, if there should be compelling reasons to do so.

In the words of the official brochure promoting the Earth Charter, the Final Version represents

> . . . *a declaration of fundamental principles for building a just, sustainable, and peaceful global society in the 21st century. It seeks to inspire in all peoples a new*

---

12   See the prior reference.

13   WWW.EARTHCHARTER.ORG/FILES/RESOURCES/BULLETIN%20JUNE%201999.DOC.

sense of global interdependence and shared responsibility
for the well-being of the human family and the larger
living world. It is an expression of hope and a call to
help create a global partnership at a critical juncture in
history. [14]

The text includes:

- A Preamble proposing a vision, analysis, and challenge for our contemporary world situation

- Four fundamental principles structures as headings for Parts I, II, III, and IV

- Four initial Main Principles that represent broad commitments and articulated in Part I

- Twelve more Main Principles, articulated in Parts II, III, and IV and required to implement the four broad commitments stated in Part I

- Sixty-one supporting principles under each of the sixteen Main Principles, to give them concrete direction

- A Conclusion entitled "The Way Forward"

The full list of principles may be found in the actual Earth Charter document, included in an Appendix toward the end of this book. We will return to examine these in a later chapter. For the moment, let us simply list the four fundamental principles at the heart of the Earth Charter, which in turn provide headings for Parts I, II, III, and IV. They are:

- Respect and Care for the Community of Life
- Ecological Integrity

---

[14]   THE EARTH CHARTER BROCHURE, p. 2.

- Social and Economic Justice
- Democracy, Nonviolence, and Peace

With this final version of the Earth Charter, the Initiative process entered its second phase, namely promoting the Charter among all peoples in all aspects of their lives. In order to plan and coordinate all major activities relating to the Earth Charter's implementation, the Earth Charter Commission formed a new international Steering Committee. This happened on June 29, 2000 at the Peace Palace in The Hague, and with the support of Queen Beatrix of the Netherlands. Presently this body includes the following co-chairs and members:

CO-CHAIRS

- Kamla Chowdhry, India
- Yolanda Kakabadse, Ecuador
- Ruud Lubbers, Netherlands
- Steven Rockefeller, United States of America

MEMBERS

- Wakako Hironaka, Japan
- Maximo Kalaw, Philippines (*deceased*)
- Alexander Likhotal, Russia
- Wangari Maathai, Kenya
- Mohamed Sahnoun, Algeria
- Severn Cullis-Suzuki, Canada
- Rick Clugston, United States of America

THE EARTH CHARTER'S VALUES

Environmentalists and scholars of global ethics alike have had a tremendous impact on the values underlying the Earth Charter's Main Principles. In the Earth Charter, for the first time in contemporary human history, the environment is no longer perceived exclusively in relation to human needs. This represents a dramatic move away from the pervasive utilitarian perspective of today's modern Western industrial society with its culture of consumerism.

As Thomas Berry has expressed in many of his writings over the last thirty years, the natural world is not a collection of objects. Rather it has intrinsic value of its own. The challenge of our time is to recognize the fact that there is no discontinuity between the human and the non-human world. Environmental rights assume a new perception through the work of Berry, with the emphasis placed on the fact that the human community must accept "Earth as a single integral community, with every being having inherent value and corresponding rights according to its mode of being."[15]

With the environmental movement, the great spiritual traditions of the world have emphasized some highly significant points.

- The natural world has value in itself.

- There is no discontinuity between the human and the non-human.

- Greed and destruction of the natural world are condemned. Religious rituals should celebrate the wonders of creation and the interconnection of the human and the natural world.[16]

---

15   Thomas Berry, "The Challenge of our Times," EARTH ETHICS, Fall/Winter 1997-98, p. 29.

16   Kusumita P. Pedersen, "Environmental Ethics in Interreligious Perspective," in Summer B. Twiss and Bruce Grelle, eds., EXPLORATIONS IN GLOBAL ETHICS: COMPARATIVE RELIGIOUS ETHICS AND INTERRELIGIOUS

In particular, the World Wide Fund (WWF) has made a great impact. In 1986 in Assisi, Italy, the WWF brought together for the first time in history five of the major world religions to declare how their own traditions cared for the natural world. What ensued were the Assisi Declarations, where religion and the environment were seen interconnected and humanity was seen as called to safeguard Earth.

This vision can be best summarized in the words of Father Serrini, OFM Conv., who stated the following on October 27, 1986.

> *We are convinced of the inestimable value of our respective traditions and of what they can offer to re-establish ecological harmony: but, at the same time, we are humble enough to desire to learn from each other. The very richness of our diversity lends strength to our shared concern and responsibility for our Planet Earth.*[17]

The awareness of the rich diversity of all forms of life is what has led many religious leaders to actively incorporate the natural world in their rites. For example, in Africa the Zimbabwean Institute of Religious Research and Ecological Conservation (ZIRRCON) and some African Independent Church Leaders (called "prophets") are incorporating ecology into their baptismal rites. When the person baptized confesses her or his ecological sins, in response there is an actual

---

DIALOGUE (Boulder, CO: Westwiew Press, 1998). The major points cited here are extracted from some of the main ideas in the book.

17   Mario Collarini, OFM Cap, *et al.,* ASSISI PROFEZIA DI PACE 27 OTTOBRE 1986 (Assisi: Casa Editrice Francescana, 1987). p. 50 (Elisabeth Ferrero's translation from the Italian).

planting of trees, in turn connected to a Eucharistic ceremony.[18]

The contemporary natural sciences, especially the new cosmology arising from physics and biology, have also been major influences on the ideas and values of the Earth Charter. In particular, the astrophysicist Brian Swimme has had a great impact not only on helping us to understand in lay terms the concept of an expanding universe, but also in experiencing the *feeling of awe* for a universe where every form of expression is intimately related to all other forms and where every form is different, has a core of its own, and exists both for its own sake and for the life of the community.[19]

In this drama of life we humans cannot simply take what we need from the natural world and discard our waste as mere objects unconnected to ourselves. Rather we humans are called to awareness of our wonderful transformative journey, and we have the responsibility to safeguard the whole ecosystem, while celebrating it in spiritual rituals, in all forms of art, and in the passing of seasons.

Spirituality is what both Swimme and Berry say occurs when we humans understand and feel deeply the sacredness of all life forms – for example, the sacred character of how plants transform the energy of the sun and the minerals of Earth for our nourishment and for the nourishment of all life forms.

---

18   Libby Bassett, ed., EARTH AND FAITH: A BOOK OF REFLECTION FOR ACTION (New York: Interfaith Partnership for the Environment, UNEP, 2000), p. 27. The entire book is an excellent resource for ecology and religion.

19   Thomas Berry and Brian Swimme, THE UNIVERSE STORY: FROM THE PRIMORDIAL FLARING FORTH TO THE ECOZOIC ERA: A CELEBRATION OF THE UNFOLDING OF THE COSMOS (San Francisco: Harper San Francisco, 1994).

The soil, the plants, and the animals all become sacred in a very special way; and in turn they are an important source of spirituality for us humans.

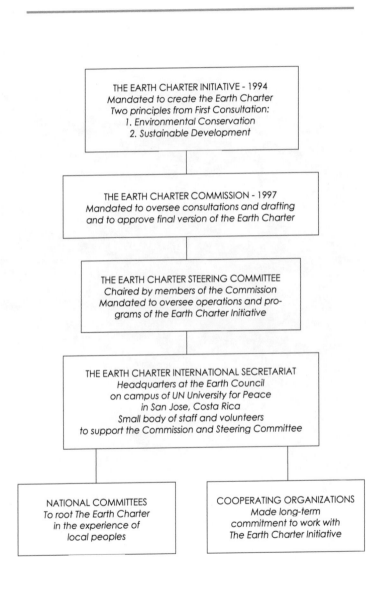

THE EARTH CHARTER INITIATIVE - 1994
Mandated to create the Earth Charter
Two principles from First Consultation:
1. Environmental Conservation
2. Sustainable Development

THE EARTH CHARTER COMMISSION - 1997
Mandated to oversee consultations and drafting
and to approve final version of the Earth Charter

THE EARTH CHARTER STEERING COMMITTEE
Chaired by members of the Commission
Mandated to oversee operations and pro-
grams of the Earth Charter Initiative

THE EARTH CHARTER INTERNATIONAL SECRETARIAT
Headquarters at the Earth Council
on campus of UN University for Peace
in San Jose, Costa Rica
Small body of staff and volunteers
to support the Commission and Steering Committee

NATIONAL COMMITTEES
To root The Earth Charter
in the experience of
local peoples

COOPERATING ORGANIZATIONS
Made long-term
commitment to work with
The Earth Charter Initiative

4

COMMENTARY ON PREAMBLE:

INTRODUCING

THE EARTH CHARTER

T he the Earth Charter -- in its process of consultation around the globe as a people's treaty -- has experienced many changes in wording, thus reflecting the shared values of the people around the globe who have taken ownership of this important text.

STRUCTURE OF THE EARTH CHARTER

As we have seen, the first *Benchmark Draft* of the Earth Charter, prepared in Rio de Janeiro in March 1997, consisted of 18 principles preceded by 4 paragraphs which stated the need for a global ethic and then elaborated further in its principles. The wording was simple and poetic, at times with clarity and brevity.

Then *Benchmark Draft II* of the Earth Charter, was released one year later -- in April 1999. This second draft became a longer document with a more defined structure: a Preamble consisting of 6 paragraphs, followed by 12 Principles and

Fundamentals, and then 9 Guidelines for Implementing Sustainability -- all together 21 principles.

But during the years that followed, there seemed to be no consensus about the number of principles or their length. Steven Rockefeller, Chairperson of the Drafting Committee, stated in a Progress Report that there had been much discussion about the length of the Earth Charter and warned:

> *If the Charter is to be widely perceived as a substantive document, it must address many more issues than can be compressed into twelve principles of one sentence each. When the legitimate interests and concerns of scientists, environmental NGOs, the peace movement, the women's movement, religious organizations, indigenous peoples, business, governments, educators, and many others are taken into consideration, the Charter principles have to be expanded. If the fundamental interests and concerns of these groups are not addressed in a way that they believe is meaningful, they will not support the Charter, and it will fail as document with a universal significance.*[1]

At last, the final version of the Earth Charter was complete. It was then presented in two forms:

- an abbreviated document consisting of the Preamble and 16 General Principles

- a full document with the Preamble, the 16 General Principles, plus 61 Supporting Principles and a Conclusion titled "The Way Forward"

---

1   THE EARTH CHARTER DRAFTING COMMITTEE PROGRESS REPORT, July 1998, p.3.

In referring to the full document, the four main parts, whose titles reflect what we will call "Fundamental Principles," are listed in Roman numerals as Part I, Part II, Part III, and Part IV. What are described as sixteen "Main Principles" gathered under these four headings are listed in Arabic numbers as Principles 1, 2, 3, etc., through to 16. Then what we call "Supporting Principles" under each Main Principle are listed alphabetically as a, b, c, etc., with the list starting anew under each Supporting Principle. (See the actual document in the Appendix for how this appears visually.)

Let us now begin a reflective commentary on the full document, beginning with the Preamble.

THE PREAMBLE

Ruud Lubbers, a major force in the development of the Earth Charter, rightly noted that the document was born out of awareness by the peoples of the Earth that a series of deficits clearly existed in the process of achieving global interdependence. These deficits included social, environmental, democratic, and security concerns. To address these concerns in a holistic way, there was needed a document that would represent "a symbiosis of governments, business and civic society."[2]

---

2   Rudd Lubbers, "A Just, Sustainable, and Participatory Society," in EARTH FORUM, On-line Conference, April 1999, p. 1, available at www.earthforum.org. The most important and inspiring work written on the major notions and issues in the Earth Charter as they are included in other documents and proposals around the world may be found in Ruud Lubbers and Patricia Morales, GLOSSARY ON GLOBAL PRINCIPLES FOR THE EARTH CHARTER, available at www.earthcharter.org.

The Earth Charter, therefore, attempted to provide a set of moral values and a call to action towards a more just and sustainable society as well as for the democratic governance and sovereignty of peoples. Its concept of a global ethic rests on three fundamental ideas: diversity, interdependence, and responsibility.[3]

The Preamble, which states the call to a global ethic, did not exist as such in the first Draft of the Earth Charter, but the Main Principles were preceded by four short paragraphs. In the second Draft, there had been an actual Preamble very similar to the final version. It had consisted of five substantial paragraphs, four of them with headings – *Earth, Our Home; The Global Situation; The Challenges Ahead; and Universal Responsibility.* The ideas of the Preamble in the first two drafts and in the final version are basically the same.

In the final version of the Earth Charter, the Preamble starts with an overview of the present global situation and calls people

> ... *to join together to bring forth a sustainable global society founded on respect for nature, universal human rights, economic justice and a culture for peace."* It also invites people to "*recognize that in the midst of a magnificent diversity of culture and life forms we are one human family and one Earth community with a common destiny.*

The Preamble's first paragraph sets the tone for the entire document and sees the "respect for nature" as one of the essential components to bring about a sustainable society.

---

3   Steven Rockefeller, "An Introduction to the Text of the Earth Charter," EARTH FORUM, On-line conference, April 1999, p. 3, at www.earthcharter.org/files/resources/ef_rockefeller.htm .

In the Preamble, the natural world is no longer perceived in a utilitarian manner as a collection of resources simply to be used for the betterment of humanity, as unfortunately remains the perspective in the dominant contemporary form of the science of economics. Rather the text stresses *respect for nature*. This concept of respect for nature is present in most religions of the world, though consciousness of this respect is repressed by the anti-ecological culture of the consumer society.

In the second paragraph of the Preamble, this respect becomes *a sacred trust*. The concept of a sacred trust stands at the core of the "new cosmology" that is being proposed by the great ecological thinker Thomas Berry. Berry traces this new cosmology to profound insights arising from new developments in the natural sciences. In this new cosmological vision, according to Berry, we humans are called to protect the beauty and the diversity of Earth.[4]

It is important to note, however, that while the Earth Charter speaks of a sacred trust, its language when addressing ethical issues remains one of duties and responsibilities. This is a major difference between the Earth Charter and Berry's cosmological vision. This difference is perhaps reflected by the fact that, while the tone of the Preamble in Draft II expressed a profound sense of 'pathos' about the current crisis, this poetic depth was lost in the final version.[5]

---

4   Thomas Berry, THE GREAT WORK: OUR WAY INTO THE FUTURE (New York: Bell Tower, 1999), pp. 200-201.

5   In Draft II one finds "reverence for the sources of our being, we give thanks for the gift of life," which in the Final Version becomes "the resilience of the community of life" and the need to preserve a "healthy biosphere." No doubt that the drafters of the Earth Charter in the final version used more basic,

Even so, the current Preamble still reflects the new cosmological vision arising from contemporary scientific information. In this vision, we humans are clearly identified as within the *"evolving universe."*

Mary Evelyn Tucker adds that this cosmological perspective

> ... *gives us a comprehensive perspective to revaluate what we are doing to the planet and how we are going to manage to restrain our destructive habits, harness our creative energies, and reconfigure human earth relations in a more constructive manner. A new balance is needed lest we destroy ourselves and many other life forms in the process.*[6]

The Preamble communicates a strongly felt urgency for us humans to change not simply our way of thinking but also of living. In particular, the third paragraph traces contemporary environmental devastation and socio-economic suffering to *"the dominant patterns of production and consumption."*

Moreover the Preamble stresses two fundamental concepts present throughout the document: 1) our interconnectness; and 2) our universal responsibility to live as a global community of life for ourselves and for future generations. To live these concepts is the real challenge.

Lastly, towards the end of the Preamble we find the following inspiring words so full of wisdom and pathos.

---

concrete terms in the attempt to appeal to the greatest number and variety of people.

6   Mary Evelyn Tucker, "Reflections on the Earth Charter," EARTH FORUM, On-line conference, April 1999, p. 2, at www.earthcharter.org/files/resources/ef_tucker.htm.

The spirit of human solidarity and kinship with all life is strengthened when we live with reverence for the mystery of being, gratitude for the gift of life, and humility regarding the human place in nature.

Let us now in the following chapters examine the principles that follow the Preamble.

5

COMMENTARY ON PART I
RESPECT AND CARE FOR THE
COMMUNITY OF LIFE

Under the first heading or first Fundamental Principle of respect and care for the whole community of life, there are gathered the first four Main Principles that the document identifies as "broad commitments" of the entire the Earth Charter. Under each Main Principle in this Part I, as in Parts II, III, and IV as well, there are listed several Supporting Principles.

PRINCIPLE 1
Respect Earth and life in all its diversity

Listed under this first Main Principle are two Supporting Principles:

a. *Recognize that all beings are interdependent and every form of life has value regardless of its worth to human beings.*

By recognizing that every form of life has value, this Supporting Principle moves away from the modern utilitarian and anthropocentric view of the natural world. It claims that all forms of life have value whether or not they are useful to humans. In the cosmological vision articulated by Thomas Berry, humans are those beings in whom Earth has come to consciousness, through whom it has reached its climax, and whose awareness embraces the entire act of creation. Presumably that does not mean, however, that we cannot defend ourselves against threats to human life from elements of the natural world, but we should do so with special care for the whole ecosystem.[1]

In a subsequent article on the Earth Charter, Duncan Taylor made the important point that Principle 1.a. (and also later Principle 5.d.) decries the current development model's elimination of biodiversity as well as the loss of species and genetic diversity through agribusiness and bioengineering. From the perspective of the Earth Charter, serious questions need to be asked about whether we can justify the genetic manipulation of natural seeds and even human genetic experimentation.[2]

Also commenting on the Earth Charter, Iain Benson argued we are called "to evaluate whether there is validity to this endless application of technology that human beings seem to

---

1   Thomas Berry, THE DREAM OF EARTH (San Francisco: Sierra Club Books, 1988). Brian Swimme has elaborated this concept in his works. See Brian Swimme, THE UNIVERSE IS A GREEN DRAGON (Santa Fe, NM: Bear and Co., 1985). See also Thomas Berry and Brian Swimme, THE UNIVERSE STORY: FROM THE PRIMORDIAL FLARING FORTH TO THE ECOZOIC ERA: A CELEBRATION OF THE UNFOLDING OF THE COSMOS (San Francisco: Harper San Francisco, 1994).

2   Duncan Taylor, "The Earth Charter: Subverting the Expansionist World View," in EARTH FORUM, On-line conference, April 1999, p. 5, at www.earthcharter.org/files/resources/Bulletin%20June%201999.doc.

have taken to themselves" and that there must be a "stance of caution with respect to manipulating an order that is, in some respects, given."[3]

b. *Affirm faith in the inherent dignity of all human beings and in the intellectual, artistic, ethical, and spiritual potential of humanity.*

This next Supporting Principle affirms the dignity of human life. Because of their inherent dignity, humans must not be treated as means but only as ends in every aspect of life, including "the intellectual, artistic, ethical, and spiritual potential of humanity."

The human person is central in the Earth Charter, and in this respect this document may be seen as a continuation of the rights of the human person, proclaimed in the United Nations' Declaration of Human Rights. As such, the Earth Charter represents what has been called "the next step in the history of human rights."[4]

Although affirming the value of all beings even apart from their use-value to humans, the Earth Charter clearly stands apart from a non-humanistic cosmology, in which humans would have no more rights than those of all other species and ecosystems, with moral obligation due equally to all parts of Earth. Sometimes such a non-humanistic cosmology is called "ecocentrism."

---

3   David Bernard and Iain Benson, "The Earth Charter Draft Document," EARTH FORUM, On-line Conference, April 1999. p. 2, at www.earthcharter.org/files/resources/ef_bernard.htm.

4   Willis S. Guerra, "On Environmental Rights and the Earth Charter," EARTH FORUM, On-line Conference, April 1997. p. 1, at www.earthcharter.org/files/resources/Bulletin%20June%201999.doc.

An ecocentric perspective would give the same value to all forms of life, and would put humans, animals, and plants on the same plane. In an ecocentric ethics, every part of the biotic community of life would have the same dignity and rights as humans. Such a position is difficult to maintain, however, even in practical terms. In reality, we need to accept some kind of biological ordering that grants humans greater dignity, yet not one that is separate from other forms of life.[5]

PRINCIPLE 2

Care for the community of life
with understanding, compassion, and love.

This second Main Principle defines humanity's call to "*care for the community of life.*" Note that the main terms used here to describe this care are "*understanding, compassion and love.*" Under its heading are two Supporting Principles:

a.   *Accept that with the right to own, manage, and use natural resources comes the duty to prevent environmental harm and to protect the rights of people*

This Supporting Principle describes caring for the community of life in language traditionally associated with stewardship of the natural world, and it employs the traditional ethical language of rights and duties. While accepting the *right of humans to own, manage, and use natural resources*, the sub-principle adds the *duty* to *prevent environmental harm and to*

---

5   Although ecocentrism can be almost seen as an absurdity if we were to simply ask, "*Does a human being have the same rights or dignity of a rock?*", one nonetheless cannot forget the value of all sentient and non-sentient beings. The 'dominion over' perspective rather than a perspective of 'care for' Earth threatens to lead to the annihilation of humans and all other forms of life.

protect the rights of people. In addition, it still uses the anthropocentric language of *resources.*

The language of stewardship contains significant limitations. As the pioneering eco-feminist thinker Elizabeth Dodson Gray has noted, stewardship is

> . . . *still steeped in hierarchy and paternalism. It takes for granted that we <u>know</u> what is right to do. Stewardship assumes that we both perceive and understand the intricate web of life which is complexly organized into ecosystems -- of which we humans are constituent parts.*[6]

The worldview of stewardship represents a serious limitation within the Earth Charter. This reflects the still predominant masculine bourgeois European and European-American Protestant view of humankind in relationship to Earth, a view sometimes found also in other Christian traditions as well as in other world religions. By contrast, the Vietnamese Buddhist Thich Nhat Hanh says "What we most need is to hear within ourselves the sound of Earth crying."[7]

b.   *Affirm that with increased freedom, knowledge, and power comes increased responsibility to promote the common good.*

This supporting principle stresses the *freedom* and the *power* that humans have to bring about a sustainable way of life. But the emphasis is on our *responsibility* as individuals, as a nation, as well as a global society on how we use and manage

---

6   Elizabeth Dodson Gray, "Come Inside the Circle of Creation: The Ethic of Attunement," a paper presented at The SECOND INTERNATIONAL CONFERENCE ON ETHICS AND ENVIRONMENTAL POLICIES, held at University of Georgia, April 5-7, 1992, p. 3.

7   Thich Nhat Hanh, as quoted by Elizabeth Dodson Gray in the paper just mentioned, p. 10.

resources. Moreover, all persons have a duty to protect and preserve the environment. Stressing that our responsibility increases with our advances in *freedom, knowledge, and power*, the principle ends with the accent on the *common good*, a reminder that we are ONE community of life.

PRINCIPLE 3

Build democratic societies that are just, participatory, sustainable, and peaceful

In this third Main Principle, there is a call to action on behalf of a comprehensive social and ecological vision. In this vision, societies that seek to be truly democratic need also to be grounded in justice, to ensure participation of all, to become ecologically sustainable, and to find paths of peace.

a. *Ensure that communities at all levels guarantee human rights and fundamental freedoms, and provide everyone an opportunity to realize his or her full potential.*

In this Supporting Principle, the Earth Charter affirms the modern cry for human freedoms. That understanding which defines human rights in terms of freedom and opportunity refers to what is codified in the initial articles of the United Nations Universal Declaration of Human Rights, proclaimed by the UN General Assembly in 1948. These are sometimes called "political and civil rights" or alternately the "first generation" of human rights.

b. *Promote social and economic justice, enabling all to achieve a secure and meaningful livelihood that is ecologically responsible.*

This second principle reflects what is sometimes called the "second generation" of "economic and social rights," which

82

are codified in later articles of the United Nations Universal
Declaration of Human Rights.

While ecological concerns raise what might be called a third
generation of human rights, we cannot build ecological societies if we violate the fundamental first and second generations of human rights. The struggle to abolish tyranny and
oppression, and the struggle to ensure ecological well-being
are closely related. The more developed countries have the
responsibility to help with the economic development of developing countries, and to do so in an ecologically responsible manner, in order to ensure a sustainable economic livelihood for all peoples.

PRINCIPLE 4
*Secure earth's bounty and beauty
for present and future generations.*

This principle of intergenerational equity is one of the four
Main Principles of the Earth Charter. The emphasis here is
on the duty of humankind to ensure that future generations
will have enough natural resources and that the biosphere of
the planet will not be severely and irrevocably damaged, and
on the importance of cultural traditions that can support this
intergenerational relationship. Again the document creatively
balances and integrates both ecological and humanistic perspectives.

Deeply moving is the fact that the concept of *beauty* is introduced alongside the concept of *bounty*. This ties in with one
of the first principles of the Earth Charter, namely Principle
1a, which holds that every form of life has intrinsic value and
needs to be appreciated in itself and not only for its utilitarian
economic value to humans.

a. *Recognize that the freedom of action of each generation is qualified by the needs of future generations.*

This first supporting principal affirms the responsibility of present generations to future ones. It reminds us of the Native American criterion of "seven generations," in which all social policies are judged by how they will affect the children seven generations from now. Our friend Macgregor Smith tells us that among some Native Americans the criterion of "seven generations" was applied by wise and senior women, the so-called "Council of Grandmothers" – a branch of government that does not seem to be present in any modern political structure. This supporting principal also reminds us of the long range commitment of Mediterranean olive farmers who for thousands of years have planted olive trees with the full knowledge that they themselves would never live long enough to see the trees bear fruit. They have planted the trees not for themselves but for their grandchildren and for more remote future generations.

b. *Transmit to future generations values, traditions, and institutions that support the long-term flourishing of Earth's human and ecological communities.*

This Supporting Principle reminds us that the commitment of present generations to future generations requires adequate cultural supports, found in our values, traditions, and institutions. We need to ask ourselves whether indeed our values, traditions, and institutions support this intergenerational commitment. If they fail to support it, then they need to be reformed to provide more adequate expressions. It seems clear that our attitudes, values, traditions, and even institutions must indeed change in order to manage our natural resources frugally and to safeguard them wisely for the children of the future.

6

COMMENTARY ON PART II

ECOLOGICAL INTEGRITY

Having established in Part I the "four broad commitments" of the Earth Charter, Part II elaborates additional Main Principles that are seen as necessary to fulfill these broad commitments. The first four of these additional Main Principles are gathered in Part II, which is titled "Ecological Integrity."

PRINCIPLE 5

Protect and restore the integrity of earth's ecological systems with special concern for biological diversity and the natural processes that sustain life

The first Main Principle contained in Part II is numbered 5, following the prior four in Part I. Main Principle 5 deals with humanity's need to protect and restore land, forests, marine life, and various native species, and not to deplete non-renewable resources like fossil fuels. The accent in this principle is on *biological diversity*. The concept of biological diversity was one of the key issues in The Convention on Biological Diversity, in 1992.[8] Ecosystems are the basis of life on the planet; therefore, their value must be constantly kept in mind by applying a conservation-based approach to the use of natural resources. Humans must *protect* and *restore* Earth's biological diversity.

In the document, Main Principle 5 has six Supporting Principles listed under it. These Supporting Principles address: a) sustainable development; b) natural and biosphere reserves; c) endangered species and ecosystems; d) threats from non-native, genetically modified, and harmful organisms; e) renewable resources; and f) non-renewable resources. Here is the document's full statement of the 6 Supporting Principles for Main Principle 5:

a. *Adopt at all levels sustainable development plans and regulations that make environmental conservation and rehabilitation integral to all development initiatives.*

b. *Establish and safeguard viable nature and biosphere reserves, including wild lands and marine areas, to protect Earth's life support systems, maintain biodiversity, and preserve our natural heritage.*

c. *Promote the recovery of endangered species and ecosystems.*

---

8   The Convention on Biological Diversity (1992) was one of the key agreements adopted at the Earth Summit in Rio in 1992. It stressed the fact that humans, as they strive for economic development, need to learn how to use biological resources in a way that minimizes their depletion. Otherwise species will become extinct. The year before, in 1991, the joint IUCN/UNEP/WWF report entitled CARING FOR EARTH: A STRATEGY FOR SUSTAINABLE LIVING, stressed that, in order to improve the conditions of the people on the globe, genetic diversity needed to be preserved and the use of species and ecosystems had to be sustainable.

d. *Control and eradicate non-native or genetically modified organisms harmful to native species and the environment, and prevent introduction of such harmful organisms.*

e. *Manage the use of renewable resources such as water, soil, forest products, and marine life in ways that do not exceed rates of regeneration and that protect the health of ecosystems.*

f. *Manage the extraction and use of non-renewable resources such as minerals and fossil fuels in ways that minimize depletion and cause no serious environmental damage.*

In supporting Principle d, there is specific reference made to the need of eradicating non-native or organically modified organisms -- an important point to which the Preamble had already made mention, but restated here with the addition of preventing the introduction of such organisms. This emphasis denotes the concern of the Earth Charter about biotechnology and its techniques of changing the DNA or genetic structure of plants and animals.

Much food in the Unites States and in most developed countries today, with the exception of organic produce, comes from seeds that have already been genetically engineered. The major problem that humanity faces from such biotechnological interventions is that at the present time we do not know what harm that these modifications might bring to us humans and to the rest of the planet.

PRINCIPLE 6

Prevent harm as the best method of environmental protection and, when knowledge is limited, apply a precautionary approach.

Main Principle 6 reiterates and expands the precautionary approach that we must employ in order to prevent harm. Under it, there appear five Supporting Principles: a) avoiding environmental harm even when we lack definitive scientific knowledge; b) placing the burden of proof on those who propose suspect activities, and making them liable for any harm; c) addressing the cumulative, long-term, indirect, long-distance, and global consequences of such activities; d) preventing pollution, especially from radioactive, toxic, or other hazardous substances; and e) avoiding military damage to the environment. Here are the five Supporting Principles as stated in the document.

a. *Take action to avoid the possibility of serious or irreversible environmental harm even when scientific knowledge is incomplete or inconclusive.*

b. *Place the burden of proof on those who argue that a proposed activity will not cause significant harm, and make the responsible parties liable for environmental harm.*

c. *Ensure that decision making addresses the cumulative, long-term, indirect, long-distance, and global consequences of human activities.*

d. *Prevent pollution of any part of the environment and allow no build-up of radioactive, toxic, or other hazardous substances.*

e. *Avoid military activities damaging to the environment.*

Supporting Principle 6a specifically states that, when we do not have enough information or when the information is inconclusive, we must use caution to prevent harm. This is an extremely important point, especially since so much genetic manipulation, both with food and with humans, is already occurring today without clear or conclusive information about the consequences. This is one of the most positive contributions of the Earth Charter, and it is placed at the very heart of this section on how we must deal with life.

Iain Benson agrees on the importance of this principle and adds that

> . . . *this idea of caution, of prudence . . . needs to become much more widely acted upon, and not only with respect to the kind of technological developments that the Earth Charter speaks to but I think increasingly we are going to see that it is necessary with respect to human ecological developments as well. . . . This is a very difficult concept to make widely understood today, where we have become adept, seemingly, in molding ourselves to technology.*[9]

Supporting Principle 6c argues systemically that decision making processes must be mindful of possible *long-term effects* and *global consequences*. The systemic thinking that the Charter is calling humans to employ in their decision making process is one of its fundamental points and defines a precondition for truly living in a sustainable way.

The fragmentation of disciplines today in our contemporary educational system, where, for example, the sciences are separated from philosophy and humanistic disciplines, cannot possibly prepare the kind of leadership that we need to bring about the transformation that the Earth Charter is heralding. Our education must be truly interdisciplinary.[10]

---

9   Iain Benson and David Bernard, "The Earth Charter Draft Document," EARTH FORUM, April 1999, p. 2, at www.earthcharter.org/files/resources/ef_bernard.htm.

10   See Benson again for his discussion on the need today of an interdisciplinary education in order to bring about the global changes that are needed. pp. 2-3.

Although we may perceive and accept our differences, Dodson Gray argues that we do not truly understand what it means to live "within an interconnected system." She adds:

> *We have a hard time thinking systemically, partly because many of these systems are so vast, but also because all our training teaches us to break problems down into "manageable" parts, rather than to see them and deal with them as a whole. Our formal education consists of experiencing knowledge divided up into departments and specialties.*[11]

Systemic thinking is what the Earth Charter says that we need when we make social and ecological decisions. Every living and non-living part of the planet, and even of the cosmos, needs to be taken into account.

To be a good decision, every decision that we make must be guided by the principle of the common good of the whole system. If a decision is good for the corporation but not for its environment, then it is a bad decision that we will come to regret. If a decision is good for humans but not for trees or tundra or permafrost, it is a bad decision. If a decision is good for men but not for women, then it is a bad decision that we will live to regret.[12]

Supporting Principle 6d calls for the prevention of *pollution.* Here the document calls governments and corporations to take a preventive approach in order to minimize and prevent discharges of harmful substances in our land, our forests, our

---

11   Elisabeth Dodson Gray, "Come Inside the Circle of Creation: The Ethic of Attunement," a paper presented at the SECOND INTERNATIONAL CONFERENCE ON ETHICS AND ENVIRONMENTAL POLICIES, held at University of Georgia, April 5-7, 1992, p. 7.

12   See the prior reference, p. 20.

water, and our air. In Supporting Principle 6b, whenever it is argued that no harm will be caused *the burden of proof* needs to lie with those who propose questionable activities.

Adopt patterns of production, consumption, and reproduction that safeguard earth's regenerative capacities, human rights, and community well-being.

Main Principle 7 gives the specifics on how we are to act economically in order to protect and restore the ecological systems of Earth. The focus of this principle is on how we are going to achieve sustainable development by engaging in activities of *production* and *consumption* that are not harmful to Earth. This requires effective new ways of optimizing resources and efficiency in how we *reduce, reuse and recycle* natural resources. Thus, governments, corporations, and consumers alike must engage in activities that are responsible and with benefits to all.

Under this Main Principle, there are listed six Supporting Principles which address: a) limiting materials and waste in production and consumption; b) using energy conservatively and efficiently, including turning to renewable energy sources; c) promoting environmentally sound technologies; d) including the full social and ecological costs of production; e) ensuring universal healthcare including responsible parenting; and f) adopting lifestyles based on quality and sufficiency in a limited world. Here is the full statement from the document of these six Supporting Principles:

a. *Reduce, reuse, and recycle the materials used in production and consumption systems, and ensure that residual waste can be assimilated by ecological systems.*

b.   *Act with restraint and efficiency when using energy, and rely increasingly on renewable energy sources such as solar and wind.*

c.   *Promote the development, adoption, and equitable transfer of environmentally sound technologies.*

d.   *Internalize the full environmental and social costs of goods and services in the selling price, and enable consumers to identify products that meet the highest social and environmental standards.*

e.   *Ensure universal access to health care that fosters reproductive health and responsible reproduction.*

f.   *Adopt lifestyles that emphasize the quality of life and material sufficiency in a finite world.*

In Supporting Principle 7b, we are reminded not to misuse *energy.* Energy is essential for sustainable development. Further, this principle calls us to substitute as much as possible for non-renewable energy sources with renewable ones like wind and solar.

Perhaps no principle in the document would have such deep economic impact as this one. The shift in energy systems from non-renewable fossil fuels, which are highly polluting, to non-polluting and renewable sources is a foundational change required for an ecological civilization. But major economic forces are currently resisting this change.

For example, although solar energy technologies are advancing rapidly, the government of United States of America, reflecting the political influence of oil, coal, and gas companies, provides major tax subsidies to the fossil-fuel industry but refuses to do the same for the solar energy industry.

Similarly in the United States the automobile and airline industries, both highly polluting in their use of fossil fuels, receive massive federal tax subsidies, while more efficient and less polluting rail systems, including urban light rail systems, receive very little governmental support and are constantly under political attack.

Supporting Principle 7c states that we must develop *environmentally sound technologies* that protect the environment, use non-renewable resources, do not pollute, and recycle most wastes.

Supporting Principle 7d calls for goods and services to reflect in their prices the true environmental and social costs. This is an extremely important issue. When someone on the East Coast of the United States buys a pound of grapes at the supermarket, does the 1.75 USD price include the real cost of the fossil-fuel pollution due to its transportation from California, or the basic human rights and needs of the migrant worker who picked the grapes? And what about the fact that the land on which the grapes are grown may well suffer depletion in its nutrition due to this type of mono-culture. Generally the answer to such questions is "no." In contemporary economic "science," such costs are labeled "externalities" and are not considered worthy of being included in "market price."[13]

---

13   Mono-culture is the practice widely used today by farmers who, instead of growing a variety of crops, concentrate on growing one type of vegetable or fruit. This process impoverishes the land which gives less and less. Consequently the farmer 'fertilizes' more and more with harmful chemicals. For an important work on the need for market prices to reflect all environmental and social costs, see Robert Costanza, *et al.*, AN INTRODUCTION TO ECOLOGICAL ECONOMICS (Boca Raton, Florida: St. Lucie Press, 1997). This in the essential link between economics and ecology.

Supporting Principle 7e supports universal access to health care that *fosters reproductive health and responsible reproduction.* This reflects a concern for women's well-being also elaborated in Main Principle 11. Here the Earth Charter emphasizes responsible patterns of *reproduction.* Education is one of the most important ways to ensure women and girls' sexual and reproductive health.

Some have reportedly criticized the Earth Charter by claiming that its use of the phrase "reproductive health" implicitly supports abortion. In response, Mirian Vilela, Executive Director of the Earth Charter's International Secretariat, has explicitly stated that the phrase "reproductive health" in the Earth Charter does not refer to abortion and she denies that the Earth Charter by using this phase implicitly supports abortion. As confirmation for Ms. Vilela's statement, the Earth Charter International Secretariat has issued an official commentary on Principle 7.e., from which we quote the following excerpt:

> *Some groups charge that all references to reproductive health care imply acceptance of abortion. This is not correct. The Earth Charter takes no position for or against abortion. (June, 2002)*

We need to distinguish between the general medical area of "reproductive health" (similar to respiratory health, cardiovascular health, etc.) and specific "policies" that may be proposed for this area of health. Those who are opposed to abortion may consistently criticize reproductive health "policies" that include abortion, but one needs not thereby be opposed to reproductive health – especially when reproductive health is today so threatened by widespread plagues of sexually transmitted diseases and particularly HIV-AIDS. Indeed Georgetown University Hospital in Washington DC, located in a major Catholic university, houses a "Center for Reproductive Health" which is actually a center for Natural Family Planning and which clearly does not support abortion. Therefore, it appears to us a false claim to declare that the Earth Charter supports abortion simply because it uses the phrase "reproductive health."

Also, we need to ensure that the primary health needs of all people are met. One important point to remember is the often prohibitively high cost of drugs. Today commercially marketed drugs are not easily affordable and often are not available to those who need them. Producing affordable drugs available to all the peoples of Earth is a major responsibility of the pharmaceutical companies.

Equally important are public health programs based on prevention, especially in poorer countries afflicted by highly communicable diseases. Many diseases today can be prevented by healthy lifestyles, healthy nutrition, and proper exercise. Health, broad-based knowledge, and socio-economic development are closely interrelated.

Supporting Principle 7f emphasizes the need to improve *the quality of life* of all people. Sustainable development needs simultaneously to care for the ecosystem and to provide a way of life that serves the basic needs and fundamental dignity of all humans.

*Advance the study of ecological sustainability and
promote the open exchange and wide application
of the knowledge acquired.*

Main Principle 8 stresses the need for *the knowledge of ecological sustainability.* This principle has listed under it three Supporting Principles.

a. *Support international scientific and technical cooperation on sustainability, with special attention to the needs of developing nations.*

Supporting Principle 8a is especially important for developing countries. These countries now have the opportunity to develop in an entirely different way from the model of the old industrial world. The old industrial model has proven destructive of both social and natural ecology. By using new solar and electronic technologies, for example, developing countries can "leapfrog" over the whole modern industrial era. They can go directly to a more ecological and just societal model that is technologically even more advanced.

The emphasis on sustainable development *vis à vis* the peoples of the South was a major contribution of the Brundtland Report. One of the major faults of the Brundtland Report, however, was that it neglected to emphasize sufficiently to what extent the people of the North needed to cut down or change their patterns of economic development.[14] Duncan Taylor points out that, since the Brundtland Report, this problem of the North has grown more and more significant.

---

14   For his discussion of the shortcomings of the Brundtland report, see Duncan Taylor, "The Earth Charter: Subverting the Expansionist World View," EARTH FORUM, On-line conference, April 1999, pp. 3-4, at www.earthcharter.org/files/resources/Bulletin%20June%201999.doc.

The economies of the South will probably continue to develop in order to redress some of the wretched disparities and inequities between South and North – and offset the erosion of economic gain by the growth of population numbers – and if this growth is to occur without doing irreversible damage to the planet's ecology, then the North must drastically cut back on its current level of consumption and be increasingly willing to redefine development in terms of social justice, environmental health, and appropriate 'quality of life' indicators.[15]

But the problem of the "rich" nations of the North is also present in class terms within the "poor" nations of the South. In most developing countries, for example India, many of the middle and upper classes have models of living comparable to those of developed countries, and these models promote the same destructive models of production and consumption.

In the United States, political resistance to needed change often seems strong. Recently, for example, following the last Kyoto Conference held in November of the year 2000, the United States, one of the countries using the biggest share of Earth's fossil fuels, refused to go along with Europe in accepting any reduction of emission of gases in the atmosphere.[16] While there were problems with the treaty that could have been remedied, the total rejection by the United States was a major setback to the battle against global warming.

---

15   See the reference for Duncan Taylor in the prior note.

16   The US already in 1992 at the Earth Summit in Rio had refused to adhere to any restrictions of emission of gases in the atmosphere. The Kyoto agreement in 1997 remained a document that nobody adhered to. In 1998, at the Buenos Aires Conference the discussion centered on how to make countries adhere to the Kyoto agreement -- without any success.

Right now global warming continues at an alarming rate --
with the polar ice caps melting, the global temperature increasing, and ocean levels rising. Moreover,

> . . . recent research has pointed out that if everyone were
> to achieve the same current level of North American
> consumption, in terms of impact on planetary life-
> support systems and the ability to absorb gases, it might
> well necessitate two additional planet Earths.[17]

In order for sustainability to become a reality, scientific and
technological knowledge must be better understood and
shared. Governmental and corporate decision-makers must
rely more on the scientific community for better ways to
achieve sustainable development. Scientists also need to
employ a holistic and organic view of the universe, rather
than the now outdated mechanistic cosmology of Newton
and Descartes.[18] Further, all institutions, including corporations, need to develop and strengthen ethical codes of conduct containing both social and ecological clauses to ensure
that knowledge will not be misused or used for personal
gains and thereby hurt the human community and its wider
ecological matrix.

b.   *Recognize and preserve the traditional knowledge and spiri-
      tual wisdom in all cultures that contribute to environmental
      protection and human well-being.*

---

17   See again Duncan Taylor's discussion, p. 3.

18   Brian Swimme is an example of a leading scientist who has embraced an
      organic and holistic cosmology. See his THE HIDDEN HEART OF THE
      COSMOS: HUMANITY AND THE NEW STORY (Maryknoll, NY: Orbis Books,
      1996).

Supporting Principle 8b addresses the *traditional knowledge and spiritual wisdom* of indigenous people. We in the industrial world need to recognize and learn from their holistic values, their nature-oriented lifestyles, and their deeply ecological spirituality. In addition, these cultures often possess holistic scientific knowledge about the planet we live in. This knowledge needs to be recognized and used in our decisions concerning the protection of the environment and of humans as well.

c. *Ensure that information of vital importance to human health and environmental protection, including genetic information, remains available in the public domain.*

In Supporting Principle 8c, the Earth Charter calls specifically for *genetic* information to be publicly available, in order to have an open and public examination of the scientific findings in this fast advancing field. This is an important point in light of the exploding amount of research in the field of genetics.

7

COMMENTARY ON PART III

SOCIAL AND ECONOMIC JUSTICE

I n Part III of the Earth Charter, we enter the entire area of human activities with regard to economics and sustainable development as the focus shifts to our global responsibilities for developing countries, women, the young, and indigenous peoples.

PRINCIPLE 9

Eradicate poverty as
an ethical, social, and environmental imperative.

The language of Main Principle 9 is the strong language of "duty," with the moral imperative to eradicate poverty. In its three Supporting Principles, the tone is one of rights, although the term "right" is not always used. Every person "ought" to have access to an equitable education and the appropriate resources for a sustainable life.

Steven Rockefeller notes that the Earth Charter does not see the eradication of poverty as an end in itself, for he claims that the document argues that

> *. . . economic activities should serve the goal of full hu-*
> *man development. The goal is human development in*
> *the fullest sense . . . and the opportunity for human de-*
> *velopment must also be pursued in a manner that is*
> *consistent with the flourishing of Earth's ecological sys-*
> *tems."*[1]

Poverty has many facets to it, both at the local level as well as globally. The changes needed must start with international efforts supporting local initiatives. Developing countries need technological, material, and financial support from the rest of the world, in order for their economies to be integrated in the global economy. But the assistance needs to support new models of development that cooperate with nature and em-power whole communities of local people. The danger, how-ever, is that the "developed" world will simply export models of technology that are clearly destructive of natural and social ecology. So this is a complex and controversial process.

a. *Guarantee the right to potable water, clean air, food security,*
   uncontaminated soil, shelter, and safe sanitation, allocating
   the national and international resources required.

In Supporting Principle 9a, the Earth Charter specifies the right to clean *water* and *air, food security, soil* free from harmful chemicals, *shelter,* and *sanitation.* These are the rights of all human beings. All these elements are perceived as essential for sustainable living. Water is the first in the list of rights, especially because of the incredible number of people in the world who do not have access to potable water and conse-quently millions of people in developing countries suffer dis-

---

1   Steven Rockefeller, "An Introduction to the Text of the Earth Charter,"
     EARTH FORUM, On-line conference, April 1999, p. 4, at
     www.earthcharter.org/files/resources/ef_rockefeller.htm.

eases and die because of contaminated water. The poor people of the globe need to produce their own food and/or have the means to buy the food they need. Developed countries have often tried to eradicate poverty by sending food aid to starving populations. This is important in case of emergencies, but is not the full and long-term answer. The full and long-term answer is a development model that fosters new style of technology that supports natural and social ecology.

b.   *Empower every human being with the education and resources to secure a sustainable livelihood, and provide social security and safety nets for those who are unable to support themselves.*

Empowerment is what Supporting Principle 9b brings into focus. By having the education and the needed resources the poor will be able to support themselves and therefore have a better sense of self-esteem, be happier and lead a more productive life. This is what eradicating poverty entails.

c.   *Recognize the ignored, protect the vulnerable, serve those who suffer, and enable them to develop their capacities and to pursue their aspirations.*

In Supporting Principle 9c, the Earth Charter addresses the needs of the *ignored*, the *vulnerable*, and those who *suffer*. Among these, there are those who suffer from the many forms of genocide and racism, from forced disappearances, from natural disasters and wars, as well as refugees and the disabled. These precious people need social and economic support and protection of their human rights as well as adequate health. It is a global responsibility to see that local governments are able to and indeed do provide those in such situations with the needed support.

Ensure that economic activities and institutions at all levels promote human development in an equitable and sustainable manner.

In this Main Principle and its four Supporting Principles, specific recommendations are listed which seek to ensure businesses, governments, commercial trading, multinational corporations, and the international financial institutions (e.g., the World Bank, the International Monetary Fund, and regional development banks) do not support a development model that is linked to the abuse of human rights and to ensure that they do support a development model that is *equitable and sustainable.*

We need to keep in mind here that all our natural resources are limited, and this situation of limits cannot change no matter how advanced our technologies become. Long-term equity and sustainability will require, therefore, that the overconsumption of the "developed" countries be reduced AND that the consumption of developing countries be increased. This is equity. Global economic actors need to promote ways to share in an equitable and sustainable manner natural resources and education.

a. *Promote the equitable distribution of wealth within nations and among nations.*

In Supporting Principle 10a, the Earth Charter calls for the equitable distribution of *wealth.* This must become a global commitment on the part of individuals as well as governments. The modern industrial development model being promoted by multinational corporations and the international financial institutions appears to be fostering just the opposite: a greater division between the rich and the poor, with much of the middle class increasingly in an insecure position. We need alternative development models that favor structures of technological design and capital flow that are specifically designed to cooperate with nature and to empower local communities. Gratefully there are important new experiments in this alternative path of development underway in many parts of the planet.

b.   *Enhance the intellectual, financial, technical, and social resources of developing nations, and relieve them of onerous international debt.*

Supporting Principle 10b refers to the needs of *developing countries* and our responsibility to relieve them of their international *debt.* There is a great urgency in helping developing countries to join the global economy. Their international debt must be dealt with in such a manner so that their repayment capacity is greater than their actual repayments and interest; otherwise they will never be able to grow.

Relieving international debt for many poor nations is also a matter of justice. Frequently these debts were contracted by corrupt and even dictatorial governments that were not elected democratically but rather imposed their regimes on local people by military force. Then not infrequently large sums of the original capital were stolen from the people by corrupt elites and even deposited out of the country in personal accounts. These debts were often made at the insistence of First World banks, particularly in the United States, that were desperate to find ways to loan out so-called "petrodollars," that is capital deposited in these banks by governments of the OPEC (Organization of Oil Producing Countries) cartel.

Decades later, many heavily indebted countries have repaid the amount of the principal over and over (in some cases ten or fifteen times!), but high interest rates have left them still deeply in debt. This is a modern version of the old situation of oppressed workers whose wages were never sufficient to pay their families' bills for company housing and food from the company store. Thus the US folk song "Sixteen Tons" sang the lament of coal miners in early industrialization: "Another day older and deeper in debt. I owe my soul to the company store."

c.   *Ensure that all trade supports sustainable resource use, environmental protection, and progressive labor standards.*

In Supporting Principle 10c, the Earth Charter insists that *trade* agreements and practices must support *sustainable resource use, environmental protection, and progressive labor standards*. As mentioned earlier in the document, business needs to concentrate on a precautionary approach and encourage environmentally friendly technologies that support sustainable development.

Further, international trade agreements and business practices need to support social codes to defend workers and the wider social community. Included in these codes needs to be the right of workers to free association, that is, the right to form unions. In certain cases, First World companies have been accused of supporting business practices in which unions are denied, politically manipulated, or even repressed, and local trade-union leaders are even assassinated.

In this Supporting Principle, the document implicitly denounces all child labor and all forms of discrimination in reference to employment and occupation as well as the reality of "sweatshops" and even slave labor, especially of women and children, found in certain parts of the world.

d. *Require multinational corporations and international financial organizations to act transparently in the public good, and hold them accountable for the consequences of their activities.*

In Supporting Principle 10d, international business and banking organizations are warned to act *transparently* and be *accountable* for the consequences of their actions. Corrupt practices are implicitly condemned; and there is a call for business, commerce, and banking to engage in fair practices across the planet.

PRINCIPLE 11

Affirm gender equality and equity as prerequisites to sustainable development and ensure universal access to education, health care, and economic opportunity.

Main Principle 11, which addresses *gender equality and equity*, brings into focus the human rights of women and girls, how women need to participate actively in society, and the need to strengthen families. Presumably equality refers to the equal dignity of all genders. It is interesting that the issue of women's rights appear immediately after the principle that deals with poverty.

The issue of women's rights achieved an important impetus in 1995 at the Fourth World Conference on Women, held in Beijing, China. More than 180 governments and thousands of women's groups gathered and approved the Beijing Platform for Action. The Platform declared that "women have an essential role to play in the development of sustainable and ecologically sound consumption and production patterns and

107

approaches to natural resource management."[2] It added that "the strategic actions needed for sound environmental management require a holistic, multidisciplinary and intersectoral approach. Women's participation and leadership are essential in every aspect of that approach."[3]

The Charter reaffirms and upholds the right to a safe and healthy environment as the basis for a transformative and sustainable society. The Earth Charter emphasizes that one crucial way to bring about long-term sustainability is to allow women to come to the foreground.

In 1997, the Boston Research Center for the 21st Century hosted a gathering of international women leaders to reflect on the Earth Charter.[4] As Soon-Young Yoon reported at the meeting,

> *Women are on the forefronts of environmental management. They select seeds, produce food, carry water, and are the main health caretakers of the family. Women manage the micro-ecology of the household and they are key decision-makers in production, reproduction, and consumption. At the same time, women do not have*

---

2   REPORT OF THE FOURTH WORLD CONFERENCE ON WOMEN, Beijing, 4-15 September 1995), as found in the "Platform of Action (Chapter I, Number 1) under Section K entitled "Women and the Environment," par. 246. The full report may be found at www.un.org/womenwatch/confer/beijing/reports/

3   See the prior reference, par. 251.

4   Their comments were published in WOMEN'S VIEWS ON THE EARTH CHARTER (Cambridge, MA: Boston Research Center for the 21st Century, 1997). The Boston Research Center is an international peace institute founded by Daisaky Ikeda, a Buddhist peace activist. One of its main goals is to help to bring about a global ethic for the 21st century by fostering dialogue among scholars and activists all over the globe. For more information, contact the Center at www.brc21.org.

equal access to the legal, political, technological, or
natural resources to do their jobs. Although in many
parts of the world women produce more than 80 percent
of the food, they own less than one percent of the land.[5]

Moreover, most of the women leaders who gathered in Boston concluded that reproductive health is a fundamental prerequisite for the exercise of all the other rights. Women need to be supported and assisted in exercising responsible fertility, especially in the era of HIV-AIDS.

The *gender equality and equity* that the Earth Charter upholds will empower women and allow them to be a strong force to combat poverty and to bring about a sustainable way of life for all. Women need to participate and take part in the decision making processes of their own institutions and government. Countries must work towards a partnership of the sexes.

This Main Principle on gender has listed under it three Supporting Principles.

a.   *Secure the human rights of women and girls and end all violence against them.*

In Supporting Principle 11a, there is a call to end all *violence* against women. Gender-based violence must end. The Earth Charter emphasizes *all* violence, in other words violence in the home as well as in public life, whether it is physical, sexual, or psychological. We might add that wars are especially dangerous to women, who regularly become targets with rape, enforced prostitution, and sexual slavery.

---

5   Soon-Young Yoon, "A Bill of Rights for Mother Nature", WOMEN'S VIEWS ON THE EARTH CHARTER, p. 58.

b. *Promote the active participation of women in all aspects of economic, political, civil, social, and cultural life as full and equal partners, decision makers, leaders, and beneficiaries.*

In Supporting Principle 11b, the *participation of women* is underlined for all aspects of life. Education and training will allow women a certain autonomy and ensure consequently greater participation in the life of the community.

c. *Strengthen families and ensure the safety and loving nurture of all family members.*

In Supporting Principle 11c, the emphasis is on *the family*. For most cultural traditions, the family is perceived as the basic unit of society, and therefore needs protection. Part of this defense of family, we might add, is protection for new mothers after childbirth.

PRINCIPLE 12

Uphold the right of all, without discrimination, to a natural and social environment supportive of human dignity, bodily health, and spiritual well-being, with special attention to the rights of indigenous people and minorities.

Main Principle 12 highlights the need to battle against discrimination in the multiple areas of race, color, sex, sexual orientation, religion, language, and national, ethnic, or social origin. In addition, it especially highlights attention to indigenous people and minorities who often have special forms of spirituality and unique ways of life.

a. *Eliminate discrimination in all its forms, such as that based on race, color, sex, sexual orientation, religion, language, and national, ethnic, or social origin.*

Supporting Principle 12a calls for the elimination of all forms of *discrimination* -- racial, religious, ethnic, sexual, etc. -- as well as of discrimination in education and against the languages spoken by minorities. Minorities have the right to their cultures and their religions as well as their languages.

We are all familiar with the struggle against discrimination, which is older than the more recent ecology movement. But it is heartening to see the ongoing battle against discrimination emphasized here and linked to ecology. One example of the link between "race" and ecology is the reality of "environmental racism," in which racial minorities often find themselves especially victimized by ecological devastation. For example, in the United States frequently toxic waste dumps are located in minority communities.

b. *Affirm the right of indigenous peoples to their spirituality, knowledge, lands, and resources, and to their related practice of sustainable livelihoods.*

The rights of the indigenous people are clearly emphasized in Supporting Principle 12b. One dramatic example of the plight of indigenous peoples in maintaining their unique ways of living was seen in the participation of indigenous peoples in the 1998 and 1999 International Conferences on Spirituality and Sustainability, held in Assisi, Italy and sponsored by both Saint Thomas University of Miami, Florida and the Center for Respect of Life and the Environment of Washington, DC.

At both of these gatherings, indigenous peoples of the North American continent who were present contended with great passion that their economic way of life, consisting of the killing of baby seals for their fur and flesh, was not against animals' rights but rather was part of their traditional culture and of their traditional economy and that, therefore, their actions could not be considered inhumane.

Consequently the representatives of indigenous peoples present appealed to those working on the Earth Charter to accept their special way of life, even though many of the participants of the conferences were opposed to the killing of baby seals. As a result of indigenous peoples' interventions at those conferences and at other gatherings that considered the Earth Charter, significant changes were made in the final wording of the Earth Charter so that the document might be inclusive of all the peoples of Earth.

c.   *Honor and support the young people of our communities, enabling them to fulfill their essential role in creating sustainable societies.*

In Supporting Principle 12c, the Earth Charter calls for our communities to *honor and support young people*. This is an important point since the Earth Charter is truly a people's treaty and uses a "bottom up" strategy that must be inclusive of all. Young people are very much a part of this "bottom up" strategy, for they are the seeds of the future.

As Maximo Kalaw said "What is most important is that the people own the Charter, not the states or the United Nations. We need to mobilize people so that their influence is felt."[6]

So much of the consultation process involved children of all ages, who were invited to discuss the Charter and to take ownership of it. As a matter of fact, part of the Earth Charter Initiative is the "Youth Initiative," providing support for initiatives of young people. Around the globe there have been

---

6   Maximo Kalaw, as quoted by Helen Marie Casey in "Dialogue on the Earth Charter," WOMEN'S VIEWS ON THE EARTH CHARTER, p. 64.

many initiatives involving children in relation to the Earth Charter. The need to increase the participation of the youth had already been addressed in the United Nation's Agenda 21.[7]

In Costa Rica, for example, middle school children played a vital role in devising their own Earth Charter. In many other countries changes in curricula were made with the suggestions and by the initiatives of young people. In Japan, the UN Student Association of Japan will include the Earth Charter as a topic of discussion at the World Youth Congress in 2002.

In the United States, the Education Development Center (EDC), which is working to promote employment with youth as a preparation for the Youth Employment Summit (YES) in 2002, held in 1997 a focus group meeting of US teachers to incorporate the Earth Charter in school curricula. The resulting list of sustainable development teaching objectives has been widely circulated and hopefully it will become a vital part of children's education.[8]

The Australian Earth Charter National Committee has been one of the most active national committees in educating the youth about the Charter's principles. They have developed extensive material for grammar and high schools.[9]

---

7   United Nations Conference on Environment and Development, AGENDA 21 (Rio de Janeiro: UNCED, 1992), Principle 12. c. The full text is available at www.un.org/esa/sustdev/agenda21.htm.

8   See the Earth Charter Initiative, www.earthcharter.org/education/.

9   The Australian Earth Charter Committee (www.earthcharter.org.au) has been developing the Earth Charter workbooks for different subjects. Each section has a main theme, followed by background, activities and outcomes. For further information contact Brendan.Mackey@anu.edu.au.

d. *Protect and restore outstanding places of cultural and spiritual significance.*

In addition to its earlier Supporting Principles addressing adults who represent the human present and youth who represent the human future, the Earth Charter here addresses the legacy of the human past by defending places of cultural and spiritual significance.

One cannot help but recall the recent destruction of precious Buddhist memorials by the Taliban in Afghanistan. Even worse, we might recall the historical charges that fanatical Christians more than a millennium ago destroyed a great part of the ancient library of Alexandria in Egypt, and that some three hundred years later the remaining part was reportedly destroyed by fanatical Muslims.

How precious are *outstanding places of cultural and spiritual significance*, and how important to preserve them for the future.

8

P art IV of the Earth Charter is a call to action for individuals, communities, institutions, and governments both at the local and global levels to achieve a truly democratic way of life. Thus democracy and ecology are seen here as partners. In Part IV, there are four more Main Principles, numbered 13 to 16. They focus on democratic institutions (13), formal education (14), respect for all life (15), and a culture of peace (16). Let us now examine each of these principles, and the Supporting Principles that inform them.

PRINCIPLE 13

Strengthen democratic institutions at all levels, and provide transparency and accountability in governance, inclusive participation in decision-making, and access to justice.

Main Principle 13 delineates the main components of *democratic governance.* At all levels, it calls for transparency and accountability, and highlights inclusive participation in decision making and access to justice. These elements are essential for constituting democratic governance.

Under this Main Principle, there are six Supporting Principles: one on the right of everyone to information (a); another on participation in decision making (b); yet another on the multiple freedoms necessary for a democratic way of life (c); one more on democratic judicial processes which also protect the environment (d); another on the need to eliminate corruption (e); and a final one on strengthening local communities so they can protect the environment (f).

a.   *Uphold the right of everyone to receive clear and timely information on environmental matters and all development plans which are likely to affect them or in which they have an interest.*

In Supporting Principle 13a, the Earth Charter emphasizes the right to *information*, particularly in relation to the environment. All individuals have a right to access whatever information and communication might be relevant to their lives, in both the environmental and other areas. The media plays a major role in this.

An example of the suppression of information happened in Tampa, Florida, in the United States, in 1997. Two journalists, Steve Wilson and Jane Akre, were dismissed by Fox Television Stations reportedly for their refusal to keep quiet their findings concerning an artificial hormone, BGH, given to cows to increase milk production -- with possible severe harms to humans.[1]

---

1   According to reports, Steve Wilson and Jane Akre, after struggling with
    Fox executives to have aired their story about the dangers of BGH, were

116

b. *Support local, regional, and global civil society, and promote the meaningful participation of all interested individuals and organizations in decision making.*

In recent times, both locally and globally, there has been a growing emphasis on the role of "civil society," that is, the regions of social organizations outside the sphere of the great state and corporate actors that have such enormous influence on the destiny of our planetary society. In particular during the past few decades, there has been an explosion of what are called "non-governmental organizations," more popularly known as NGOs.

The United Nations (UN) gives official recognition to NGOs, allowing many of them to make interventions at UN conferences and in many UN processes. NGOs, particularly by their work though the UN, have enabled ordinary citizens from civil society to make their views felt upon the stage of world history.

c. *Protect the rights to freedom of opinion, expression, peaceful assembly, association, and dissent.*

With the right of information, comes the right to express one's opinion, to assemble peacefully, and to voice dissent. Supporting Principle 13c lists these as essential elements for ensuring democratic governance and abolishing the abuse of power. Included in the right of peaceable assembly and identified as such in other UN documents is the right to form trade un-

---

dismissed in December of 1997. Subsequently they sued Fox Television Stations and after a five-weeks trial in 2000 they won their suit. For the complete story of this as well a view of the original video that Fox refused to air, see www.foxbghsuit.com.

ions. Trade unions are among the most broad-based NGOs on the planet and have enormous potential for promoting democracy, justice, peace, and ecologically sustainable development.

d.   *Institute effective and efficient access to administrative and independent judicial procedures, including remedies and redress for environmental harm and the threat of such harm.*

In Supporting Principle 13d, the Earth Charter emphasizes the right to *judicial procedures* as well as *remedies and redress for environmental harm.* Every person is equal before the law. This right cannot be violated either at the national or international level, and includes the right to judicial access on environmental matters. Moreover, people need to be compensated in the case of pollution and environmental damage.

e.   *Eliminate corruption in all public and private institutions.*

In Supporting Principle 13e, there is a call to eliminate corruption –from money laundering to bribery. All forms of corruption are condemned and must be wiped out for a global society to prosper. Perhaps of special concern should be the ability of unaccountable transnational actors to hide money in offshore banking havens to avoid paying taxes.

f.   *Strengthen local communities, enabling them to care for their environments, and assign environmental responsibilities to the levels of government where they can be carried out most effectively.*

The Earth Charter places great emphasis here on the most basic level of local communities, where so much can be done. Sustainable development cannot be some abstract concept uprooted from real communities of local peoples. That is why we prefer to speak not only generally of "sustainable development" but also more specifically of "sustainable communities."

We need to bring about change in our own communities, in the places where we work and live. We need to share our dreams among ourselves and to encourage one another to actively participate in the decision-making processes of our local governance. This will empower us as local citizens and will identify responsible adult role models for local youth. Local communities can best care for their own environments, since they have the most intimate knowledge about their own regions.

PRINCIPLE 14

Integrate into formal education and life-long learning the knowledge, values, and skills needed for a sustainable way of life.

Main Principle 14 states that, under democratic governance oriented to a sustainable way of life, education needs to play a vital role, including *formal education and life-long education.* The Earth Charter sees education as one of the fundamental ways to transform society. The right to education for everyone has been one of the Main Principles heralded in the Earth Charter and in previous international documents as well. Parents are the most responsible agents for helping their children to achieve the best education they can, but the responsibility extends also to society as a whole.

There are four Supporting Principles for Main Principle 14. They address the following themes, all in relation to education for sustainable living: a) education of all, especially children and youth; b) the arts, humanities, and sciences; c) mass media; and d) moral and spiritual formation.

119

a.   *Provide all, especially children and youth, with educational opportunities that empower them to contribute actively to sustainable development.*

Supporting Principle 14a states that all, especially *children and youth*, must have the best educational opportunities. This implies no educational discrimination against women and girls. Moreover, governments must fight against all possible obstacles in order to foster the educational development of their youth. Implicit here is that all forms of abuse, especially against girls, must be abolished. Environmental education programs need to be moved to center stage in all schools around the globe and integrated across all curricula.

As part of life-long learning, there needs to be in-service environmental training for all professions. One example is how the International Council for Adult Education (ICAE) in Canada used the Earth Charter to help people to better understand their own jobs and how they could better contribute to the health of Earth.[2]

On May 17-19, 2001 in Wiscasset, Maine, an important academic symposium, *Teaching for the Environment in Higher Education -- the Promise of the Earth Charter* raised important ethical and aesthetic questions with regard to the environment and to the role of education.[3] More such academic symposia are needed to plan for the implementation of Main Principle 14.

b.   *Promote the contribution of the arts and humanities, as well as the sciences in sustainable education.*

---

2   For a rich list of national activities, see the Earth Charter Initiative website at www.earthcharter.org/country.

3   See the prior reference.

Supporting Principle 14b emphasizes the important role played by *the arts and humanities* in sustainable education, in addition to the sciences.

The Earth Charter recognizes the importance not only of reason and logic towards the attainment of sustainable education but also the enormous transformation brought about by songs, music, poetry, dance, and stories. As part of the Earth Charter Initiative, there has been the Earth Charter Art Project, with pictures and poetry by children from Algeria, Russia, Uruguay, and the USA.[4]

An interesting gathering supporting this principle took place in Vermont on the shores of Lake Champlain on Sept. 9, 2001. Entitled for love of Earth, A Celebration of the Earth Charter, it brought together an abundance of music, art, dance and stories — all celebrating with symbolic power the meaning of the Earth Charter. Steven Rockefeller shared the Earth Charter Creation stories and led the participants in a choral reading of the Earth Charter principles.[5]

In regard to the role of the sciences, we have the great example of the masterful book by Thomas Berry and Brian Swimme, The Universe Story.[6] The book gathers into a lyrical and even mystical story all the riches of contemporary scien-

---

4   For information on education and the creative arts, see "Education" at www.earthcharter.org.

5   Again, see the Earth Charter Initiative for abundant examples at www.earthcharter.org.

6   Berry, Thomas & Swimme Brian. THE UNIVERSE STORY: FROM THE PRIMORDIAL FLARING FORTH TO THE ECOZOIC ERA: A CELEBRATION OF THE UNFOLDING OF THE COSMOS (San Francisco: Harper San Francisco, 1994).

tific knowledge about the universe. We know this story as the new cosmology.

c. *Enhance the role of the mass media in raising awareness of ecological and social challenges.*

Supporting Principle 14c affirms that *mass media* is a fundamental component in bringing about transformative education for sustainable living. Media needs to be given complete freedom to fulfill its essential role for informing our global society about the requirements of our new ecological path.

It is distressing to note, however, that certain media commentators in the United States even deny that there is a threat of global warming. Gratefully other sectors of the media are playing a more helpful role, but there is much more to be done.

d. *Recognize the importance of moral and spiritual education for sustainable living.*

Lastly, Supporting Principle 14d recognizes *the importance of moral and spiritual education.* This affirmation is a major contribution of the Earth Charter, for so much of modern Western Culture has tried to strip the whole world, and especially education, of any spiritual content, and sometimes of any ethical content.

This is an especially important principle, particularly in the face of a modern Western secularization that has attempted to undermine and erode the great spiritual traditions of Earth. How impoverished is modern culture, and consequently how ecologically destructive, when it becomes blind to the awesome power of the sacred as revealed through the natural world.

The deep respect that we all need to have for one another's spirituality, and together for the sacredness of all creation, is one of the essential components of the celebration of diversity — including biodiversity and cultural diversity -- stands at the core of the message of the Earth Charter.

PRINCIPLE 15

Treat all living beings with respect and consideration.

Main Principle 15, so fundamental in the Earth Charter, was already a part of Benchmark Draft II. All the living species of Earth, and within every species each individual living creatures, are precious and require our respect and consideration. Under it are listed three Supporting Principles.

a. *Prevent cruelty to animals kept in human societies and protect them from suffering.*

Steven Rockefeller has noted that this principle is crucial for non-human living creatures because presently international law, while recognizing the moral standing of species (as in protecting endangered species), does not give moral or spiritual value to individual non-human living beings. He emphasizes that "The Earth Charter calls for respect and care for all individual living beings as well as species." But Rockefeller carefully adds: "the intention in this regard is not to oppose all consumption of non-human species, because such consumption has historically been necessary for human survival, but the Earth Charter does condemn the unsustainable and cruel use of non-human species." In other words, this principle of the Earth Charter does not say that we all need to become vegetarians.[7]

However, this principle does implicitly condemn the practices of modern industrial or factory models of animal farming. For example, in this cruel model chickens are jammed into crowded coops with no room even to move. In turn, they are flooded with light all the time so that they eat and become fatter faster. Further, their beaks are clipped so that they will not hurt one another in such small confinement. And then they are constantly given hormones and antibiotics, which in turn enter the bodies of those who eat them.[8] Such practices, fundamentally unhealthy and cruel, are rejected by the Earth Charter and need to be abolished.

b. *Protect wild animals from methods of hunting, trapping, and fishing that cause extreme, prolonged, or avoidable suffering.*

Supporting Principle 15b requires that wild animals also be treated in an humane manner. This does not mean that there should be no hunting, trapping, or fishing. Indeed many non-human living beings are also themselves hunters and fishers. But the principle does ask that such activities be conducted in such a way as to minimize the suffering of these animals. Ancient peoples always had a deep respect and reverence for the animals that they hunted, trapped, or fished.

---

7   Steven Rockefeller, "An Introduction to the Text of the Earth Charter," EARTH FORUM, On-line conference, April 1999, p. 4, www.earthcharter.org/files/resources/ef_rockefeller.htm.

8   For a disturbing view of the factory model of animal farming, see the powerful video, DIET FOR A NEW AMERICA, narrated by John Robbins, and read John Robbins' equally powerful book, DIET FOR A NEW AMERICA (Walpole, New Hampshire: Stillpoint Publishing, 1987).

Many individuals who pursue such activities as a sport often manifest a deep ecological consciousness and a concern to minimize animal suffering. The real threat of cruelty to non-human animal species and to individuals within them comes more often from the commercial application of industrial models of hunting, trapping, and fishing.

c.   *Avoid or eliminate to the full extent possible the taking or destruction of non-targeted species.*

Supporting Principle 15c presumably refers to situations like the famous case of large commercial ocean fishing nets that, along with the fish they sought, also captured and killed many other species, for example dolphins and turtles. We need to cease such destructive activities and prevent them for the future.

PRINCIPLE 16
Promote a culture of tolerance, nonviolence, and peace.

Main Principle 16 elaborates the components of a global society at peace, including tolerance and nonviolence.

Tolerance, which needs to be mutual, is indispensable for understanding, solidarity, and cooperation. We human beings all need to respect each other and our differences. Only such mutual respect will bring about a strong civil society. All forms of intolerance are implicitly condemned, including racial and religious extremism. Of course, the Earth Charter here presumably speaks of respecting differences acceptable within humanity's widely agreed-upon framework of human rights and human ethics. Thus, for example, genocide could never be viewed simply a cultural "difference."

We note here the recent worldwide examples of ethnic cleansing and the emergence of neo-fascist movements, as

125

well as the survival "white supremacist" movements in the United States and Europe, and, of course, the worldwide networks of violent terrorism and global drug trafficking – all rejecting human solidarity and so destructive of tolerance, nonviolence, and peace.

Unfortunately there have been terrorists from all cultures who have appealed to religion to support their violent murder of innocent people. Such terror, however, finds no justification in any authentic religion; it is exclusively an act of evil.

As testimony to the importance of this Main Principle, it has listed under it six Supporting Principles. These address: a) understanding and solidarity among peoples; b) strategies to resolve conflicts; c) diminishment of militarization with conversion of resources to peaceful and ecological purposes; d) elimination of weapons of mass destruction; and f) recognition that peace is holistic, extending across personal, cultural, and ecological dimensions.

Under this Main Principle, there are listed six Supporting Principles.

a. *Encourage and support mutual understanding, solidarity, and cooperation among all peoples and within and among nations.*

Supporting Principle 16a holds up a vision of *mutual understanding, solidarity and cooperation* as essential elements to bring about sustainability. How important, therefore, that we develop programs of inter-cultural and inter-religious dialogue across the planet. Of special importance here is the "Dialogue among Civilizations," initiated by the United Nations, with special support from the United Nations Educational, Scientific, and Cultural Organization (UNESCO).

b. *Implement comprehensive strategies to prevent violent conflict and use collaborative problem solving to manage and resolve environmental conflicts and other disputes.*

In addition to needing solidarity and cooperation, we need to learn better how to develop comprehensive strategies to deal non-violently with both environmental and social conflicts. It is quite conceivable, indeed even probable, that in the near future we will face large scale social conflicts over limited natural resources.

Water is one dramatic example. As population expands and as water consumption is increasingly diverted to such industrial or factory models of agriculture or in the United States to luxury consumption by watering golf courses and private lawns, certain regions may well face drastic and even life-threatening shortages of water. Regional wars could easily develop over access to water.

How important, therefore, that we plan ahead to develop strategies for sharing natural resources in a way that protects their sustainability and provides equitable sharing across the entire human family.

c. *Demilitarize national security systems to the level of a non-provocative defense posture, and convert military resources to peaceful purposes, including ecological restoration.*

In our technological and globalized world, vast amounts of natural resources and human energy are increasingly spent on military equipment and activities. Meanwhile, many nations of the world lack adequate resources for meeting basic human needs like food, shelter, healthcare, and education. Religious leaders and others across the planet have regularly decried this destructive imbalance. How can we protect the military security of the peoples of Earth when so many have trouble surviving economically and when the ecological security of all is itself increasingly threatened?

Therefore, we need to develop better models of global and national governance, as well as of economic development, so that disarmament can be truly pursued in a way that increases our overall security. If we can find better ecological, economic, political, cultural, and even spiritual ways of protecting human security, then significant disarmament will indeed become feasible. Then we will be able to reduce military budgets and shift resources to the development of civic society, and especially to the needs of the poor and marginalized.

The very concept of *security systems* brings into light the fact that today we need to talk not narrowly about national security but more comprehensively about global security, which means the social and ecological security of both humankind AND the biosphere of the whole planet.

d.   *Eliminate nuclear, biological, and toxic weapons and other weapons of mass destruction.*

In Supporting Principle 16d, the Earth Charter calls for *the elimination of nuclear, biological, and toxic weapons and other weapons of mass destruction*, which implies an end to the export of toxic military wastes to developing countries, as has often been the case. (Though it is not mentioned here, we also need to stop the vast and often illicit traffic of small arms and light weapons, which fosters so many local military conflicts around the world.) Further, all states need to cease the production and use of all chemical and biological weapons. Moreover, disarmament must be done under strict international controls. As we know so tragically, recent outbreaks of international terrorism have awakened us to the potential and terrifying danger of chemical and biological weapons of mass destruction.

e. *Ensure that the use of orbital and outer space supports environmental protection and peace.*

Supporting Principle 16e insists that *outer space* needs to be used to support *environmental protection and peace*. We know, of course, that there are already gargantuan plans to militarize space. For example, many people probably do not realize that the National Aeronautic and Space Administration (NASA), the civilian space agency of the United States, is the smallest US space agency, with each military branch reportedly having its own and larger space agency. Further, there have been strong efforts to bring NASA indirectly under military dominance.

f. *Recognize that peace is the wholeness created by right relationships with oneself, other persons, other cultures, other life, Earth, and the larger whole of which all are a part.*

Supporting Principle 16f caps the Earth Charter's concern with peace by urging us to recognize *that peace is the wholeness created by right relationships with oneself, other persons, other cultures, other life, Earth, and the larger whole of which we are a part.* This broad vision of peace is reminiscent of the holistic meaning of the Hebrew word *Shalom* and the Arabic word *Salam.* (The verb "create" is used frequently in the Earth charter, but only in the literary sense of imaginative innovation, rather than in the strictly scientific sense of creation *ex nihilo.*)

In this final statement there is a summation of all the previous principles of the Earth Charter: 1) Respect and care for the community of life; 2) ecological integrity; 3) social and economic justice; and 4) democracy, nonviolence, and peace.

These all come together in a holistic vision of peace for this vast community of life within which we humans are only a small part.

Main Principle 16 with its six Supporting Principles is one of the longest in the Earth Charter. Its discursive tone conveys some of the pathos found more in the previous drafts of the document. This sense of pathos seems to have been lost in much of the final version, perhaps because of a desire to cast the text more in the legal style of UN documents. Nonetheless, Mary Evelyn Tucker appropriately states that the Earth Charter conveys the strong feeling that "peace among humans is only possible with peace with the planet," and that "the liberation of humans can only take place in conjunction with a new understanding of human-earth relations."[9]

Artists, philosophers and musicians alike have been expressing this for a long time. For example, Thomas Berry has lyrically conveyed this deep sense of community and oneness with the natural world that so many modern humans have lost. Repeatedly he has warned that, without this fundamental awareness of our communion with the very Earth of which we are a part, our spirituality becomes impoverished and even destructive.

In sum, the Earth Charter challenges us to regain and continue a sustainable life for all. These principles challenge us to move rapidly away from the environmentally destructive path of modern societies, and from the attempt to colonize the whole planet according to the anti-ecological modern imagination. Such an attempt surely threatens not only ecological,

---

9   Mary Evelyn Tucker, "Reflections on the Earth Charter," EARTH FORUM, On-line conference, April 1999, p. 3, at www.earthcharter.org/files/resources/ef_tucker.htm.

but also social and spiritual devastation. The way to viable human future is only in communion with Earth.

9

COMMENTARY ON CONCLUSION

THE WAY FORWARD

The conclusion of the Earth Charter is really a call to a very different and hopefully sustainable future. The conclusion consists of five inspirational paragraphs. The first paragraph sets the stage.

> *As never before in history, common destiny beckons us to seek a new beginning. Such renewal is the promise of these the Earth Charter principles. To fulfill this promise, we must commit ourselves to adopt and promote the values and objectives of the Charter.*

In the first line of this first paragraph, we are called to a new beginning, a *renewal.* Such a transformation, it proclaims, will require a *change of mind and heart;* and there will be tensions and difficult *choices* to make. However, the end result will be a *sustainable global society.*

This simple message is infused with an incredible amount of pathos -- especially in the first and the last paragraphs. There is a vision of strength with a sense of urgency in the conclusion of the Earth Charter. The human in this intricate web of life stands out for his/her capacity to bring about a new era.

Although the Earth Charter speaks and calls to action all segments of society, including its institutions, and governments, *the change of heart and mind* is what every single individual needs to do – to change her or his attitudes, values and ways of living.[1] The newly found strength comes from the awareness that it is *possible* to change and that we are not alone. This is the constant message of Thomas Berry:

> *If the dynamics of the universe from the beginning shaped the course of the heavens, lighted the sun, and formed Earth, if this same dynamism brought forth the continents and seas and atmosphere, if it awakened life in the primordial cell and then brought humans into beings and guided them safely through the turbulent centuries, there is reason to believe that this same guiding process is precisely what has awakened in our present understanding of ourselves and our relation to this stupendous process. Sensitized to this guidance we can have confidence in the future that awaits the human venture.*[2]

The remaining four paragraphs of the Earth Charter's conclusion, printed below, require no further commentary. We simply recommend reading their words in a reflective and meditative way.

---

1   Mary Evelyn Tucker, "Reflections on the Earth Charter," EARTH FORUM, On-line conference, April 1999, p. 3, at www.earthcharter.org/files/resources/ef_tucker.htm.

2   Thomas Berry, as quoted by Mary Evelyn Tucker in the prior reference, p. 4.

*This requires a change of mind and heart. It requires a
new sense of global interdependence and universal responsibility. We must imaginatively develop and apply
the vision of a sustainable way of life locally, nationally,
regionally, and globally. Our cultural diversity is a precious heritage and different cultures will find their own
distinctive ways to realize the vision. We must deepen
and expand the global dialogue that generated the
Earth Charter, for we have much to learn from the ongoing collaborative search for truth and wisdom.*

*Life often involves tensions between important values.
This can mean difficult choices. However, we must find
ways to harmonize diversity with unity, the exercise of
freedom with the common good, short-term objectives
with long-term goals. Every individual, family, organization, and community has a vital role to play. The
arts, sciences, religions, educational institutions, media,
business, nongovernmental organizations, and governments are all called to offer creative leadership. The
partnership of government, civil society, and business is
essential for effective governance.*

*In order to build a sustainable global community, the
nations of the world must renew their commitment to the
United Nations, fulfill their obligations under existing
international agreements, and support the implementation of the Earth Charter principles with an international legally binding instrument on environment and
development.*

*Let ours be a time remembered for the awakening of a
new reverence for life, the firm resolve to achieve*

sustainability, the quickening of the struggle for justice and peace, and the joyful celebration of life.

10

THE EARTH CHARTER

AS A NEW GLOBAL ETHIC

O ver the last three hundred years, ethics has tended to become the exclusive domain of religion, while the sciences, economics, law, and technology have dealt with the practical side of the "business of living." Furthermore, ethics has been referred almost exclusively to human beings. By contrast, the Earth Charter is proposing fundamental rights applicable to all forms of life, and is also arguing that this broader sense of ethics, rooted in an ecological vision, is indispensable for a sustainable human future. As Willis Guerra has stated, the Earth Charter needs to be understood as "a continuation to the declaration of human rights. We can conceive it as the next step in the history of human rights."[1]

1   Willis S. Guerra, "Environmental Rights and the Earth Charter," EARTH FORUM, An on-line Conference, April 6-9, 1999, p. 2, at www.earthcharter.org/files/resources/Bulletin%20June%201999.doc.

There is a great urgency for the Earth Charter, especially in light of the multiplicity and escalation of environmental, social, and spiritual problems that we confront today in our lives. This visionary document calls us to action, as a human family, to work together to solve the full range of problems before us all --- with no longer a separation between faith and reason, spirit and matter. This is a moment of real opportunity that carries within it the transformative power of those events that can change the course of history and life on Earth.

One of the major tasks and responsibilities of our times is centered on halting the immeasurable harm caused by the faulty perception of the relationship of the human to the natural world. We need to speak of the essential Earth-human relationship, and to understand what exactly this relation means in order to determine what are humans' responsibilities.

The sacred nature of all creation has deep theological roots in all religions. For example, Saint Thomas Aquinas clearly states in his *Summa Theologiae* that, because the Divine could not express itself in one single being, it created the great multiplicity of beings so that the perfection lacking in one could be supplied by the others.[2]

---

2   Thomas Aquinas, SUMMA THEOLOGIAE, I, Q. 47, Art. 1. Thomas Berry has repeatedly referred to this reference in all his writings. Saint Thomas consistently refers to the "order of the universe", and his SUMMA CONTRA GENTILES he refers to this order as "the ultimate and noblest perfection in things"(Chapter 45).

The differentiation of all species -- human and non-human, the rivers and the stars -- expresses the Divine both within the interior of human consciousness and across the order of the universe. This Divinely ordered integration of exterior and interior, personal and cosmic, is the inner law mentioned by Saint Paul in his Epistle to the Romans.[3]

The natural world is not simply a background for the human or a context into which humans are inserted. Humans are absolutely dependent upon the rest of creation not only for survival, but also for spiritual growth and identity. By experiencing nature the human experiences the divine as well. The Bible speaks again and again of the goodness and beauty of creation.

Moreover, all major religions seem to have several points of agreement in environmental ethics.

- "The natural world has value in itself and does not exist solely to serve human needs."

- "Non-human living beings are morally significant, in the eyes of God and/or in the cosmic order."

- "Greed and destructiveness are condemned."

- "Humans and non-human beings are morally significant, in the eyes of God or the cosmic order."

- "Moral norms such as justice, compassion and reciprocity apply (in appropriate ways) both to human beings and to non-human beings. The well-being of humans and the well-being of non-human beings are inseparably connected."

---

3   Romans. 4:8, cited from THE JERUSALEM BIBLE (New York: Doubleday and Company, 1966).

- "The dependence of human life on the natural world can and should be acknowledged in ritual and other expressions of appreciation and gratitude."[4]

Although each part of creation exists for itself, for its own growth and development, primarily and above all, each part exists to bring life to a single integral community and thus, to creation itself. The human cannot function independently from the rest of the universe; humans cannot exploit for their own good, because by seeking one's own well being at the expense of the wider community of life we diminish our own well-being *and* the well being of all creation, of the entire universe.

Bedrich Moldan speaks of the human dominance on the natural world as

> . . . *our magnificent contemporary feast without a price. The problem is that this price is not paid by we who enjoy the feast. It is paid by somebody else. It is paid by nature, by the global geosphere that provides us with all the essential services we need for our rich banquet.*[5]

This domination on Earth is aggravated by the fact that the carrying capacity of the planet is limited. Therefore, a utilitarian approach (the dominant ethos guiding modern Western culture) to the environment of the non-human world can only increase the disorder of the universe, with the resulting spiritual and social

---

4   Interfaith Partnership for the Environment, EARTH AND FAITH, Libby Bassett, ed. (New York: United Nations Environment Programme), p. 78.

5   Moldan Bedrich, in "Global Ethics, Sustainable Development and the Earth Charter," EARTH FORUM, An on-line Conference, April 6-9, 1999, p. 1, at www.earthcharter.org/files/resources/ef_moldan.htm.

degradation of humankind as well.[6] Greed, selfishness, instant gratification, and over-consumer-ism (only to mention some of the great social problems of today) have disturbed the natural balance of the universe and in the process have impoverished our souls and hearts. What is needed is a fundamental shift as a global society to adopt a transformative global ethic.

The solutions to our problems today are acceptable only if they are sustainable in every way. A sustainable society satisfies its needs without diminishing the prospects for future generations. We should not work for efficiency but to preserve the whole network of relationships of the humans to the non-human world. The Earth Charter presents us with a blueprint to meet the challenges before us. We must pledge a strong commitment to its principles in our attitudes, our values, and in the way we live. Institutions and governments must shift drastically from their myopic human-centered values and services to embrace the universe.

As Robert Muller has expressed it so well,

> *We are entering a thrilling, transcending, new global, cosmic phase of evolution in the line indicated by Teilhard de Chardin, the anthropologist, if the human species understands its suddenly momentous, incredibly important evolutionary role and responsibility. Existing institutions must be reformed and/or created to perform this role.[7]*

---

6   Thomas Berry, THE DREAM OF EARTH (San Francisco: Sierra Club Books, 1988), pp. 33-35.

7   Robert Muller, "The Absolute, Urgent Need for Proper Earth Government", in "Global Ethics, Sustainable Development and the Earth Charter," in

The Earth Charter heralds the vision of a transformative global ethic grounded in two fundamental principles: 1) environmental conservation; and 2) sustainable development. In this ethic, the human and the non-human live systemically in a mutually enhancing relationship. Interdependence is what the Earth Charter affirms in all its principles.

Steven Rockefeller says that the Earth Charter

> ... *is not just a document about the environment. It has been constructed with the understanding that humanity's environmental, economic, and social problems are interrelated and can only be effectively addressed with integrated global solutions.*[8]

The need, then, is for governments, institutions, and all members of civil society to work together. This is why the Earth Charter has been constructed not as an intergovernmental document, but as a people's treaty, with a bottom-up strategy, in order for dialogues and negotiations to involve *all* the peoples of Earth working toward sustainability.

The World Commission on Environment and Development's definition of sustainable development states clearly our goals as a global society in meeting

---

EARTH FORUM., An on-line Conference, April 6-9, 1999, p. 6, at www.earthcharter.org/files/resources/ef_muller.htm.

8   Steven Rockefeller, "An Introduction to the Text of the Earth Charter " in "Global Ethics, Sustainable Development and the Earth Charter" in EARTH FORUM, An on-line Conference, April 6-9, 1999, p. 2, www.earthcharter.org/files/resources/ef_rockefeller.htm.

*... the needs of the present without sacrificing the abil-
ity of future generations to meet their own needs ...
Economics and ecology must be completely integrated in
decision-making and law-making processes not just to
protect the environment, but also to protect and promote
development.*[9]

Maximo Kalaw added that in order for sustainability to become a reality we must have

*... changes in personal behavior. In other words, how
do we relate to society and how do we govern ourselves?
This question has a political dimension and, at bottom,
it has a very deep spiritual dimension . . . (and how
these values) reflect in terms of people's lives, in terms of
their livelihood, in terms of the organizations they join,
in terms of how they communicate, and in terms of the
political advocacy they undertake for the public interest.*[10]

The issue of social justice is central to sustainability. The
Earth Charter reiterates with its many "oughts" and moral
imperatives the deeply felt sense of obligation that we all
share towards the natural world <u>and</u> in providing an adequate
quality of life for all humans. In the process of becoming
sustainable, we must foster and pledge ourselves to service
and specifically to the creation of effective outreach resources
to assist especially the wider community of the poor, indigenous peoples, women, and youth.

---

9   World Commission on Environment and Development, 1987.

10   Maximo Kalaw, "Framework for the Earth Charter, " in WOMEN'S VIEWS
ON EARTH CHARTER (Cambridge, MA: Boston Research Center for the 21st
Century, 1997), p. 28.

Is sustainability still possible when so many giant multinational corporations seem to dominate so many aspects of our lives in a way that is unaccountable to the natural world? Thomas Berry strongly speaks against any giant corporations whose main goal is only

> ... to exploit the planet, with reference only to its economic value. Their products are delivered to the consumer public after convincing them that an economy based on the extraction and transformation of the components of Earth, thought of simply as 'natural resources,' is making for a better and infinitely more fulfilling life than a way of life lived within the organic ever renewing systems of the planet. The corporation has become the basis of survival of the human community. We now live in a world created by the industrial way of life with a vast number of technological controls over the natural world . . . (and) when we survey the extent to which corporations control our lives, their possession of legal rights to the use of property throughout the planet, their control over governments, the legal profession, the universities, their thought control through the public media; and when we consider their relative isolation from any political authority or cultural norms of action, we begin to realize the dimensions of the challenge before us.[11]

If we follow Berry's analysis, we conclude that wide ranges of modern Western economic systems are no longer sustainable,

---

11   Thomas Berry, "The Challenge of Our Times" in EARTH ETHICS (Washington DC: Center for Respect of Life and Environment), Fall/Winter 1997/98, p. 32.

and, therefore, we *must* search for new solutions to meet the challenge of our times.

Supporting Berry's challenge, Robert Muller, the founder of the United Nations University for Peace says that

> . . . *the world corporate community should be asked to answer how they would provide for a well-preserved planet and the well-being of all humanity, full employment, the renewal of natural resources, the long-term evolution of the planet and continuation of life on it, the real democracy of the consumers in a corporate power and wealth economy.*[12]

As Ashok Khosla has written, in order for an economy to be sustainable, it is imperative to look at how we deal with the use of our natural resources. Six billion people cannot rely on how we deal presently with our resources throughout the world.[13] New ways to use natural resources are needed. Besides the much solar, wind, micro-hydro, and biomass alternatives to the use of energy from petroleum, creative efforts must be employed in the search of alternatives in all aspects of our lives.

In India, Khosla continues, Development Alternatives have worked with a totally different kind of construction material in the building of houses. They use mud to make beautiful

---

12   Robert Muller, "The Absolute, Urgent Need for Proper Earth Government", in "Global Ethics, Sustainable Development and the Earth Charter," in EARTH FORUM, An on-line Conference, April 6-9, 1999, p. 2, at www.earthcharter.org/files/resources/ef_muller.htm.

13   Ashok Khosla, "Development Alternatives" in "Global Ethics, Sustainable Development and the Earth Charter," in EARTH FORUM, an on-line Conference, April 6-9, 1999, p. 2, at www.earthcharter.org/files/resources/ef_khosla.htm.

buildings and have developed a entire new series of roofing materials as well.[14] It is essential that technology be used in a way that will

> ... *create jobs instead of destroying them, that regenerates the environment instead of destroying it and (creates) jobs that bring meaning and dignity into the lives of people, because the technologies underlying them are basically geared to our needs and not to their own.*[15]

The Earth Charter speaks for a sustainable life for all the peoples of Earth who must feel empowered and responsible for their own lives.

Women's rights are emphasized in the Earth Charter, especially in relation to the issues of their health and economic equality. The plight of women around the globe was globally recognized at the Beijing Women's Conference in 1995. The resulting *Platform for Action* for the first time defined women's rights as human rights. Consequently women have the right to health, development, equality and peace. The Earth Charter stands firmly for gender equality because women and girls presently around the globe still need to be protected from poverty, sexual abuse, and lack of self-esteem. Susan Davis sums up the repercussions of the present condition of most women over the world today by stating that "gender equality is the prerequisite for sustainable development."[16]

---

14   See the prior reference.

15   See the prior reference.

16   Susan Davis, "Principle-Centered Evolution: A Feminist Environmentalist Perspective" in WOMEN'S VIEWS ON THE EARTH CHARTER (Cambridge, MA: Boston Research Center for the 21st Century, 1997), p. 44.

Soon-Young Yoon illustrates this concept with the crisis of gender apartheid in Afghanistan. In some Taliban-controlled territories, including Kabul, women were prevented from attending schools and work. However, the result was that the education of boys was impaired because 70% of all elementary school teachers were women. The same problem was encountered in hospitals where women had formerly rendered most of the services.[17]

The Earth Charter emphasizes the need to open our hearts and minds and create sustainable ways of living also for women, the poor, the indigenous people and the youth.

One of the most important solutions towards sustainability is the building of local communities. The concept of a global society is not contradictory to the development of local communities. On the contrary, sustainable living is only possible by promoting social and economic systems of a particular region thereby strengthening the self-reliance and responsibility of its local people who implement and maintain their systems.

Susan Darlington says that "the full potential of the Earth Charter lies in how it is perceived, interpreted, and acted on by the people in local areas throughout the world" and on how the Earth Charter's "abstract principles (will be) applied to concrete situations and begin to have an effect on the world's environment and well-being."[18]

---

17   Soon-Young Yoon in "A Healthy Self, a Healthy Society, a Healthy Planet," in "Global Ethics, Sustainable Development and the Earth Charter," in EARTH FORUM, An on-line Conference, April 6-9, 1999, p. 2, at www.earthcharter.org/files/resources/ef_yoon.htm.

18   Susan M. Darlington, "The Earth Charter and Ecology Monks in Thailand,"

Building local communities, then, with the respect for the diversity of cultures, spirituality, geography and so forth, is one of our present tasks.

No global ethic, no global community can maintain itself without affirming the vastness of the diversity of the human and non-human that comprise the globe.

The principle of diversity is fundamental in the Earth Charter and needs to be translated at the local level not only in the development of social and economic systems of livelihood, but also in affirming and celebrating the many different experiences that previous generations have transmitted to us through the arts, rituals and stories. We are told that "stories, parables, and commentaries on the precepts carry forward the wisdom of those who have come before us. Their struggles with restraint have yielded priceless insight into the realm of human nature."[19]

At times, the Earth Charter has been seen as a document consisting of principles that are too abstract and therefore do not inspire and move people to change. Donald Swearer reiterates the urgent need for the Earth Charter principles to be grounded in concrete examples of particular lives, and he emphasizes "the value of stories in our search for the principles of a universal environmental ethic, for stories are more compelling than principles no matter how praiseworthy they

---

BUDDHIST PERSPECTIVES ON THE EARTH CHARTER (Cambridge, MA: Boston Research Center for the 21st Century, 1997), p. 50-52.

19   Stephanie Kaza, "A Matter of Great Consequence," BUDDHIST PERSPECTIVES ON THE EARTH CHARTER, p. 73-75.

may be."[20] We need to carry on the wisdom of our "living elders" so that their deep humanity may encourage others by example.

The transformation to which the Earth Charter calls each of us is a kind of inner work. It is the change of mind and heart that each one of us has to bring about. In the words of Consolación Alarsas, our main task is that "our conscience must catch up to our reason, otherwise we are lost."[21]

With this personal transformation, Robert Muller sees the necessity for all the nations of the world to unite in creating a "World Union on the pattern of the European Union" -- reminding oneself of the incredible progress of the 15 nations of the European Union, which have put an end to their antagonisms and wars and have embraced a common destiny and goals. He further states that "this example is so hopeful, so powerful, so novel and inspiring that I recommend it as an outstanding guide-light for more regional communities and for the entire globe."[22]

---

20   Donald Swearer, "'Rights' because of Intrinsic Nature or 'Responsibilities' because of Mutual Interdependence?," BUDDHIST PERSPECTIVES ON THE EARTH CHARTER, p. 90.

21   Consolación R. Alaras, "A Nation's Sacred Covenant with the People's Earth Charter," in "Global Ethics, Sustainable Development and the Earth Charter," EARTH FORUM, An on-line Conference, April 6-9, 1999, p. 2, at www.earthcharter.org/files/resources/Bulletin%20June%201999.doc.

22   Robert Muller, "The Absolute, Urgent Need for Proper Earth Government", in "Global Ethics, Sustainable Development and the Earth Charter," in EARTH FORUM, An on-line Conference, April 6-9, 1999, p. 6, at www.earthcharter.org/files/resources/ef_muller.htm.

Muller's vision embraces not only humanity but all of creation when he reiterates the proposal by Barbara Gaughen-Muller

> . . . *to create a United Nature, a transformed United Nations to respond to the fundamental unity of nature of which humans are part. Humans would not dominate nature but cooperate with it and learn from it. It is probably the most advanced, timely and imaginative vision of the total, proper functioning of planet Earth.*[23]

We are truly at the dawn of a new era with tremendous possibilities. The Earth Charter calls each one of us to transformation and in the process save humankind and this wonderful planet Earth.

Thomas Berry speaks of our current crises as fundamentally spiritual in nature.[24] Our sensitivities need to recognize fully the sacred dimension of Earth. Without the awareness that all forms of life are sacred in themselves, without experiencing this, all our clean-up efforts, all changes in our lifestyles are just another form of work; they do not transform us and are not healing us. We have to change the perception of who we are, and our role *vis a vis* the rest of creation. We have to accept creation as "the communion of subjects (and) not a collection of objects."[25] Each part of creation is necessary

---

23   Robert Muller, "The Absolute, Urgent Need for Proper Earth Government", in "Global Ethics, Sustainable Development and the Earth Charter," in EARTH FORUM, An on-line Conference, April 6-9, 1999, p. 3-6, at www.earthcharter.org/files/resources/ef_muller.htm.

24   Thomas Berry. THE GREAT WORK: OUR WAY INTO THE FUTURE (New York: Bell Tower, 1999), p. 61.

25   Berry, THE GREAT WORK, p. 103.

and indispensable. If we diminish any part of this communion, we diminish our sense of the sacred.

Moreover, this transformation requires also that we experience the sense of the sacred in the history's unfolding of ideas, the arts, poetry, and literature. We also have to recapture the sacred dimension by experiencing the planet and the history of the universe. In all our institutions: commerce, law, religion, and education we must judge what inhibits or fosters the mutually enhancing relationship that humans have with the rest of Earth.

Berry reminds us that there is not an isolated human community, but one earth community.[26] We need to gather hope and strength in order to endure the pains in the days to come that such transformation will bring about.

BEGINNING WITH OURSELVES

What can each of us really do? How and where do we start?

Above all, we must bring about in our lives some kind of "voluntary simplicity" that supports ecological sustainability, social justice, and human peace.[27] This requires a great deal of inner work, as well as outer work. We need to ask ourselves: How much do we need for our well-being? We must be gentle and patient with ourselves and with others, since this is a long and complex process. Yet we also need constantly to remind ourselves that some things are not negotiable.

---

26   Thomas Berry, lecture delivered in Assisi at St. Thomas University's Study Abroad for the Earth (SAFE) program, 1993.

27   See Duane Elgin, VOLUNTARY SIMPLICITY: TOWARD A WAY OF LIFE THAT IS OUTWARDLY SIMPLE, INWARDLY RICH, Revised Edition (Tempe AZ: Dimension Books, 1993).

Here are some specific steps, hardly exhaustive, that may help us begin the long process of personal transformation:

- We can turn away as much as possible from those multi-national corporations that uproot economic life from local bioregional communities, and also support small business and local entrepreneurs who seek to care for local bioregional communities. We especially need to boycott products that are lethal to the natural world and humans.

- We can try to function within a bioregional context, i.e. live and support our bioregions by learning to recognize the crops it produces, its climate, its geography, its various forms of life.

- We can fight urban and suburban sprawl as much as possible, and choose to live in small cooperative communities, to work near our homes or even from our homes, and to develop mutually supportive relationships with people in our communities.

- We can try to use more bicycles for local transportation, walk as much as possible, and for longer travel use buses, trains, and car-pooling.

- We can try to free ourselves from dependence on agricultural mono-cultures, which are high in the use of fossil-fuel energy sources and petrochemical techniques for growing food, and instead opt for organic foods that are not from genetically engineered seeds. We can seek out such food from local growers as much as is possible, since they require less fossil-fuel energy spent in processing, transporting and marketing. We can also support community agriculture and shared crops ventures, as well as start our own organic garden or join with others who already have one.

- We can seek jobs that are not simply work that needs to be done for utilitarian purposes, or that pay well, but actually represent the 'role' that we humans are called to play in the context of all life, and that, therefore, honor the dignity of work.

- We can use as much as possible renewable resources, and follow the three R's (reduce, reuse, recycle). We can remind ourselves that technologies need to take care of their waste and not support technologies that fail to do so.

- We can avoid abusing air, soil, water, and vegetation, for otherwise we will bring about a resource deficit and destroy a living process of which we are very much a part.

- We can become involved politically in local, national, and even global movements, especially through political parties that are open to ecology, justice, and peace, and also through the many non-governmental organizations (NGO's) that take up these causes.

- We can seek to root our spiritual life in the wonder of creation, and find in creation a living echo of the Divine mystery itself.

- We can teach our children to live sustainably, especially by showing them through our own example.

- And so much more . . .

BIBLIOGRAPHY AND RESOURCES

UNITED NATIONS DOCUMENTS

1948   Universal Declaration of Human Rights

1972   Stockholm Declaration of the United Nations Conference on the Human Environment

1982   World Charter for Nature

1987   Our Common Future, Report of World Commission on Environment and Development

1987   Tokyo Declaration of the World Commission on Environment and Development

1987   United Nations Environmental Program Goals and Principles of Environmental Impact Assessment

1992   Agenda 21: Program or Action for Sustainable Development

1992   Convention on Biological Diversity

1992   Rio Declaration on Environment and Development

1995   Platform for Action from Beijing Women's Conference

WORKS DIRECTLY RELATED TO THE EARTH CHARTER

1997   Earth Charter Benchmark Draft. *San José, Costa Rica: Earth Charter Secretariat*

1999   Earth Charter Benchmark Draft II. *San José, Costa Rica: Earth Charter Secretariat*

2000   Earth Charter. *San José, Costa Rica: Earth Charter Secretariat, 2001. www.earthcharter.org*

2001   The Earth Charter Initiative: Handbook. *San José, Costa Rica: Earth Charter Secretariat. www.earthcharter.org*

2001   The Earth Charter: Status Report 1999/2000. *San José, Costa Rica: Earth Charter Secretariat. www.earthcharter.org*

Berry, Thomas. 1988. THE DREAM OF EARTH. San Francisco, CA: Sierra Club Books. *A remarkable collection of essays in which the author explains the fresh and exciting ecological vision of new scientific cosmology in which humans and the rest of nature are one in the wonder of creation. The book also creatively explores the implications of this cosmological vision for society's professions and institutions.*

Berry, Thomas & Stephen Dunn (ed.) 1991. BEFRIENDING EARTH: A THEOLOGY OF RECONCILIATION BETWEEN HUMANS AND EARTH. Mystic, CT.: Twenty-third Publications. *A series of vibrant dialogues between Thomas Berry, CP and Thomas Clarke, SJ on the spiritual implications of the new cosmology, especially from a Christian perspective but with insights that can be shared among all world religions.*

Berry, Thomas & Brian Swimme Brian. 1994. THE UNIVERSE STORY: FROM THE PRIMORDIAL FLARING FORTH TO THE ECOZOIC ERA: A CELEBRATION OF THE UNFOLDING OF THE COSMOS. San Francisco: Harper San Francisco. *A complete scientific and cultural narrative of the new cosmology that is emerging from the frontiers of contemporary science. It tells the story of the evolving universe from its very beginning to our times, and sees the entire cosmos as holistic, artistic, and even mystically sacred. The book is full of both scientific data and a broad human spirituality that truly inspires the reader.*

Berry, Thomas. 1999. THE GREAT WORK. OUR WAY INTO THE FUTURE. New York: Bell Tower. *Berry's most recent work, which brings together all his earlier work into a comprehensive cultural vision for a new civilization centered technologically and spiritually in ecology.*

Berry, Wendell. 1986. THE UNSETTLING OF AMERICA: CULTURE AND AGRICULTURE. New York: Sierra Club Books, 1996. *One of America's most prominent poets, who is also a farmer, writes eloquently about peoples and their land from profoundly ecological perspective.*

Brown, Lester R. 2001. STATE OF THE WORLD, 2001: A WORLDWATCH INSTITUTE REPORT ON PROGRESS TOWARD A SUSTAINABLE SOCIETY. New York: Norton. *A valuable publication by experts on the basic ecological threats and opportunities confronting all aspects of life on Earth. Each year the Worldwatch Institute publishes a new edition with updated data. These annual volumes are the best single summary of the global ecological situation.*

Capra, Fritjof, & Charlene Spretnak. 1984. GREEN POLITICS. New York: Dutton, 1984. *An excellent and comprehensive analysis of the worldwide attempt to develop "Green" political parties. Though focused on "Green" parties, the book has resourceful ideas for political contributions and actions by all parties.*

Carson, Rachel. 1962. SILENT SPRING. Cambridge, Mass.: Riverside Press. *This incredible and lyrical book may have been the original inspiration behind the contemporary ecological movement. Rachel Carson, then a scientist with the United States Department of Agriculture, was the first one to publicly describe the devastating effects on humans and all forms of life by the use of pesticides, particularly DDT. The author came under vicious attack from certain chemical companies, but her prophetic research has since been broadly validated.*

Casey, Helen Marie & Amy Morgante. Eds. 1997. WOMEN'S VIEWS ON THE EARTH CHARTER. Boston, Mass.: Boston

Research Center for the 21st Century. *A series of papers around the Earth Charter and women from various women leaders around the globe.*

Colburn, Theo, *et al.* 1996. OUR STOLEN FUTURE. New York: E. P. Dutton. *This book is a must for all. It reports on the horribly damaging effects of chemicals extraneously introduced into our waters and into every aspect of our lives. Colburn is the Rachel Carlson of our times.*

Christiansen, Drew & Walter Grazer (Eds.). 1996. AND GOD SAW THAT IT WAS GOOD: CATHOLIC THEOLOGY AND THE ENVIRONMENT. Washington DC: United States Catholic Conference. *An important and valuable collection of essays on Catholic perspectives for eco-theology.*

Conroy, Donald & Rodney Petersen (Eds.). 2000. EARTH AT RISK: AN ENVIRONMENTAL DIALOGUE BETWEEN SCIENCE AND RELIGION. Amherst NY: Humanity Books. *A rich collection of essays in the new dialogue between religion and science in light of the new cosmology and edited by two leaders in the field.*

Costanza, Robert, et al. 1997. AN INTRODUCTION TO ECOLOGICAL ECONOMICS. Boca Raton, Florida: St. Lucie press. *One of the leading ecological economists of today who looks at sustainable economics and what it involves.*

Davidson, Eric A. 2000. YOU CAN'T EAT GNP: ECONOMICS AS IF ECOLOGY MATTERED. Cambridge, Massachusetts: Perseus. *A book on how to live sustainably -- by a scientist who makes complex issues simple and easy to grasp.*

Dillard, Annie. 1974. PILGRIM AT TINKER CREEK. New York: Harper and Row. *A classic work by a very gifted writer touched by the natural world.*

Dillard Annie. 1983. TEACHING A STONE TO TALK: EXPEDITIONS AND ENCOUNTERS. New York: Harper & Row. *A series of personal experiences by the same gifted writer touched by the natural world.*

Bassett, Libby, John T. Brinkman, Kusumita P. Pedersen (Eds.) 2000. EARTH AND FAITH: A BOOK OF REFLECTION FOR ACTION. New York: United Nations Environment Programme. *An important book which delineates the role that religions have played in the environment and the major areas of concern today.*

Eiseley, Loren. 1978. THE STAR THROWER. New York, New York: Times Books. *A marvelous book looking at the new scientific cosmology in a way that the non-scientist can clearly understand. Making the complex seem simple, it reaches out in poetic terms to young and old.*

Fox, Matthew. 1994. THE REINVENTION OF WORK. San Francisco: Harper San Francisco. *A wonderful book which guides us in changing the way we live and our concept of work.*

Gray, Elizabeth Dodson. 1979. GREEN PARADISE LOST. Wellesley, Massachusetts: Roundtable Press. *A pioneering ecofeminist historical critique of our civilization and a rich exploration a creatively alternative path.*

Hawken, Paul, Amory Lovins, & L. Hunter Lovins. 2001. NATURAL CAPITALISM. Boston, Little, Brown and Company. *Written by some of the best minds on alternative energy systems, this book is a must for grasping the relationship of economics environment and sustainability.*

Hill, Brennan R. 1998. CHRISTIAN FAITH AND THE ENVIRONMENT: MAKING VITAL CONNECTIONS. Orbis Books: Marykoll, NY. *An ecumenical and scholarly but accessible study of the eco-consciousness in Christian history, including its Jewish roots. Especially helpful is a review of new ecologically oriented church documents from around the world.*

Korten, David. 1995. WHEN CORPORATIONS RULE THE WORLD. San Francisco: Kumarian Press and Berrett-Koehler Publishers. *Also a must to understand the power of global mega-corporations and the need for an alternative development model centered in the sustainability and control of local communities.*

Leopold, Aldo. 1949. A SAND COUNTRY ALMANAC. New York: Oxford University Press. *A classic book to explore the relationship of humans to the natural world,*

Lubbers, Ruud, & Patricia Morales. 2001. GLOSSARY ON GLOBAL PRINCIPLES FOR THE EARTH CHARTER. Available at www.earthcharter.org. *An essential book on the major ideas in the Earth Charter as they relate to all other previous documents and proposals.*

Mills, Stephanie. 1995. IN SERVICE OF THE WILD. Boston: Beacon Press. *A book full of pathos about the natural world and the role humans must play in restoring its wonder and its beauty.*

Morgante, Amy. Editor. 1977. BUDDHIST PERSPECTIVES ON THE EARTH CHARTER. Cambridge MA: Boston Research Center for the 21st Century. *A series of dialogues on how the Earth Charter relates to Buddhism. The dialogues are led by leading experts in this field.*

Rockefeller, Steven C. 1996. PRINCIPLES OF ENVIRONMENTAL CONSERVATION AND SUSTAINABLE DEVELOPMENT. Prepared for the Earth Charter Project and available at www.earthcharter.org. *An incredibly important study on International Law with documents and reports from the United Nations and non-governmental organizations.*

Ruether, Rosemary Radford. 1994. GAIA AND GOD: AN ECOFEMINIST THEOLOGY OF EARTH. San Francisco: Harper San Francisco. *A feminist theologian's perspective on our history and Western culture, in particular the role that religion and Christianity have played in its unfolding.*

Sale, Kirkpatrick. 1985. DWELLERS IN THE LAND: THE BIOREGIONAL VISION. San Francisco: Sierra Club Books. *An important text on the concept of the bio-region.*

Sheldrake, Rupert. 1988. THE PRESENCE OF THE PAST: MORPHIC RESONANCE AND THE HABITS OF NATURE. New York: Times Books. *A fascinating hypothesis of a non-reductionist or holistic interpretation of natural evolution.*

Snyder, Gary. 1984. GOOD. WILD. SACRED. Hereford, U.K.: Five Seasons Press. *A very moving book by one of the most important American poets of our times on the natural world.*

Spretnak, Charlene. 1991. STATES OF GRACE: THE RECOVERY OF MEANING IN THE POSTMODERN AGE. San Francisco: Harper San Francisco. *Written by a leading eco-feminist, this book is a fascinating exploration of the major world religions with emphasis on their contributions to ecology and justice. Contains a powerful critique of the deconstructionist school of postmodernism.*

Swimme, Brian. 1984. THE UNIVERSE IS A GREEN DRAGON: A COSMIC CREATION STORY. Santa Fe, New Mexico: Bear and Co. *A wonderful book, written by a physicist who is also very much a poet, that describes in very simple dialogues some of the most complex issues of a cosmology based on an evolving universe where humans are deeply connected to Earth.*

Swimme, Brian. 1996. THE HIDDEN HEART OF THE COSMOS: HUMANITY AND THE NEW STORY. Maryknoll, NY: Orbis Press. *An incredible book, a must for all in order to understand the new scientific data concerning the universe and the humans' role in it. Very well written, in a language simple but full of insights and passion.*

STUDY GUIDE FOR ACTION

FOR USE IN CLASSROOMS

AND BY SMALL GROUPS

First, Gather Others to Study
this Book about the Earth Charter

To be effective in support of the Earth Charter, we need to encourage others to join us in changing the way we live – to shift our lifestyles from complicity in the destructive consumer culture to promotion of a sustainable path for our families and ourselves.

One way that we can do this is by forming a group to study the Earth Charter. Such groups may be classes in a school, or small gatherings of friends or associates meeting in homes, religious institutions, workplaces, or community centers.

Second, Read Each Chapter of this Manual
and Keep a Short Personal Journal on your Reading

The group or class may wish to spend one session on each chapter of this manual, or may wish to combine several chapters for each session.

In any case, we recommend that the organizer of the group or class ask each participant to write a SHORT PERSONAL

JOURNAL, perhaps 2 pages long, after reading each assigned section. The journal may answer the following questions.

1. How did this reading affect you emotionally?

2. What new information did you learn?

3. What do you and others need to do in light of this information?

The organizer of the group may ask the participants to bring their journals to the next meeting of your group and class and to share what they have written.

Third, Develop a Personal Plan
for Responding to the Earth Charter

Either as an individual or in a group or class, develop a personal plan of response. The following suggestions may help.

1. Ponder how the Earth Charter principles fit in with your own spirituality.

2. Draw a picture, write a poem, or sing/play a song that celebrates Earth and all creation.

3. Make a list of the values in the Earth Charter that seem the most valuable to you.

4. Apply these values and principles in concrete, everyday situations.

5. Seek out elders or/and indigenous people and listen to their creation stories.

6. Look around where you are locally for examples that illustrate the Earth Charter principles.

7. Follow in the media with respect to what is happening in the environment and in the area of sustainable development.

8. Start your own organic garden, even a very small one to begin with.

9. Spend time outside in the natural world, to reconnect spiritually with its beauty and mystery.

10. Express compassion for all forms of life, including for those humans who are suffering.

Fourth, Encourage Others to Join You in Awareness and Action

Next you may wish to move toward action. Either through your group or class, or by joining with others outside your group or class, begin to implement and live the Earth Charter. The following ideas may be helpful suggestions.

1. Maintain an open channel of information in your family, and gently help the persons around you to become aware, but do so without being judgmental or imposing.

2. Share in your group with friends, family and co-workers the importance of what you are doing and ask them whether they want to join you.

3. Ask them if they wish to start an environmental club or to strengthen an existing one.

4. Organize such a club in your religious organization, in a society that you belong to, at your workplace, in school, or among some of your friends. Then gather the club for a weekly discussion on how the Earth Charter is

transforming their lives. In your group be sure to sing or play some music, and read some poetry. Art is very important for personal and social transformation.

5.   Invite your group to organize clean-up days and tree-planting ceremonies.

6.   Invite your group to start an organic garden in your religious institution, your school, or your neighborhood.

7.   Invite your group to start petitions in your area to bring about those changes that are important to your community and send them to your political representatives, school board, or your religious leadership.

8.   Invite your group to encourage all of those around you to bring about a sustainable life for all humans and reduce environmental destruction by reusing, reducing, and recycling.

9.   Invite your group to organize a concert in your area, a poetry reading, or a workshop.

10. Invite your group to study and talk about the social, economic, spiritual and moral development needed in order to bring about a sustainable way of life.

For each of the above-mentioned activities, after you have done them gather with others to share the meaning the activity had in your personal lives. Moreover, you might use a story to share the meaning, and then discuss the story in your group the meaning it has for each one of you. The same goes for pictures, poems and songs.

Whatever you do, keep studying, keep acting, and keep growing!

THE EARTH CHARTER

March 2000

(Reprinted with Permission)

PREAMBLE

We stand at a critical moment in Earth's history, a time when humanity must choose its future. As the world becomes increasingly interdependent and fragile, the future at once holds great peril and great promise. To move forward we must recognize that in the midst of a magnificent diversity of cultures and life forms we are one human family and one Earth community with a common destiny. We must join together to bring forth a sustainable global society founded on respect for nature, universal human rights, economic justice, and a culture of peace. Towards this end, it is imperative that we, the peoples of Earth, declare our responsibility to one another, to the greater community of life, and to future generations.

EARTH, OUR HOME

Humanity is part of a vast evolving universe. Earth, our home, is alive with a unique community of life. The forces of nature make existence a demanding and uncertain adventure, but Earth has provided the conditions essential to life's evolution. The resilience of the community of life and the well-being of humanity depend upon preserving a healthy biosphere with all its ecological systems, a rich variety of plants and animals, fertile soils, pure waters, and clean air. The global environment with its finite resources is a common concern of all peoples. The protection of Earth's vitality, diversity, and beauty is a sacred trust.

THE GLOBAL SITUATION

The dominant patterns of production and consumption are causing environmental devastation, the depletion of resources, and a massive extinction of species. Communities are being undermined. The benefits of development are not shared equitably and the gap between rich and poor is widening. Injustice, poverty, ignorance, and violent conflict are widespread and the cause of great suffering. An unprecedented rise in human population has overburdened ecological and social systems. The foundations of global security are threatened. These trends are perilous—but not inevitable.

THE CHALLENGES AHEAD

The choice is ours: form a global partnership to care for Earth and one another or risk the destruction of ourselves and the diversity of life. Fundamental changes are needed in our values, institutions, and ways of living. We must realize that when basic needs have been met, human development is primarily about being more, not having more. We have the knowledge and technology to provide for all and to reduce our impacts on the environment. The emergence of a global civil society is creating new opportunities to build a democratic and humane world. Our environmental, economic, political, social, and spiritual challenges are interconnected, and together we can forge inclusive solutions.

UNIVERSAL RESPONSIBILITY

To realize these aspirations, we must decide to live with a sense of universal responsibility, identifying ourselves with the whole Earth community as well as our local communities. We are at once citizens of different nations and of one world in which the local and global are linked. Everyone shares responsibility for the present and future well-being of the human family and the larger living world. The spirit of human solidarity and kinship with all life is strengthened when we live with reverence for the mystery of being, gratitude for the gift of life, and humility regarding the human place in nature.

We urgently need a shared vision of basic values to provide an ethical foundation for the emerging world community. Therefore, together in hope we affirm the following interdependent principles for a sustainable way of life as a common standard by which the conduct of all individuals, organizations, businesses, governments, and transnational institutions is to be guided and assessed.

PRINCIPLES

I. RESPECT AND CARE FOR THE COMMUNITY OF LIFE

1. Respect Earth and life in all its diversity.

    a. *Recognize that all beings are interdependent and every form of life has value regardless of its worth to human beings.*

    b. *Affirm faith in the inherent dignity of all human beings and in the intellectual, artistic, ethical, and spiritual potential of humanity.*

2. Care for the community of life with understanding, compassion, and love.

   a. *Accept that with the right to own, manage, and use natural resources comes the duty to prevent environmental harm and to protect the rights of people.*

   b. *Affirm that with increased freedom, knowledge, and power comes increased responsibility to promote the common good.*

3. Build democratic societies that are just, participatory, sustainable, and peaceful.

   a. *Ensure that communities at all levels guarantee human rights and fundamental freedoms and provide everyone an opportunity to realize his or her full potential.*

   b. *Promote social and economic justice, enabling all to achieve a secure and meaningful livelihood that is ecologically responsible.*

4. Secure Earth's bounty and beauty for present and future generations.

   a. *Recognize that the freedom of action of each generation is qualified by the needs of future generations.*

   b. *Transmit to future generations values, traditions, and institutions that support the long-term flourishing of Earth's human and ecological communities.*

In order to fulfill these four broad commitments, it is necessary to:

II. ECOLOGICAL INTEGRITY

5. Protect and restore the integrity of Earth's ecological systems, with special concern for biological diversity and the natural processes that sustain life.

   a. *Adopt at all levels sustainable development plans and regulations that make environmental conservation and rehabilitation integral to all development initiatives.*

   b. *Establish and safeguard viable nature and biosphere reserves, including wild lands and marine areas, to protect Earth's life support systems, maintain biodiversity, and preserve our natural heritage.*

   c. *Promote the recovery of endangered species and ecosystems.*

   d. *Control and eradicate non-native or genetically modified organisms harmful to native species and the environment, and prevent introduction of such harmful organisms.*

   e. *Manage the use of renewable resources such as water, soil, forest products, and marine life in ways that do not exceed rates of regeneration and that protect the health of ecosystems.*

   f. *Manage the extraction and use of non-renewable resources such as minerals and fossil fuels in ways that minimize depletion and cause no serious environmental damage.*

6. Prevent harm as the best method of environmental protection and, when knowledge is limited, apply a precautionary approach.

a. *Take action to avoid the possibility of serious or irreversible environmental harm even when scientific knowledge is incomplete or inconclusive.*

b. *Place the burden of proof on those who argue that a proposed activity will not cause significant harm, and make the responsible parties liable for environmental harm.*

c. *Ensure that decision making addresses the cumulative, long-term, indirect, long distance, and global consequences of human activities.*

d. *Prevent pollution of any part of the environment and allow no build-up of radioactive, toxic, or other hazardous substances.*

e. *Avoid military activities damaging to the environment.*

7. Adopt patterns of production, consumption, and reproduction that safeguard Earth's regenerative capacities, human rights, and community well-being.

a. *Reduce, reuse, and recycle the materials used in production and consumption systems, and ensure that residual waste can be assimilated by ecological systems.*

b. *Act with restraint and efficiency when using energy, and rely increasingly on renewable energy sources such as solar and wind.*

c. *Promote the development, adoption, and equitable transfer of environmentally sound technologies.*

d. *Internalize the full environmental and social costs of goods and services in the selling price, and enable consumers to identify products that meet the highest social and environmental standards.*

e. *Ensure universal access to health care that fosters re-productive health and responsible reproduction.*

f. *Adopt lifestyles that emphasize the quality of life and material sufficiency in a finite world.*

8. Advance the study of ecological sustainability and promote the open exchange and wide application of the knowledge acquired.

   a. *Support international scientific and technical cooperation on sustainability, with special attention to the needs of developing nations.*

   b. *Recognize and preserve the traditional knowledge and spiritual wisdom in all cultures that contribute to environmental protection and human well-being.*

   c. *Ensure that information of vital importance to human health and environmental protection, including genetic information, remains available in the public domain.*

III. SOCIAL AND ECONOMIC JUSTICE

9. Eradicate poverty as an ethical, social, and environmental imperative.

   a. *Guarantee the right to potable water, clean air, food security, uncontaminated soil, shelter, and safe sanitation, allocating the national and international resources required.*

   b. *Empower every human being with the education and resources to secure a sustainable livelihood, and provide social security and safety nets for those who are unable to support themselves.*

c. *Recognize the ignored, protect the vulnerable, serve those who suffer, and enable them to develop their capacities and to pursue their aspirations.*

10. Ensure that economic activities and institutions at all levels promote human development in an equitable and sustainable manner.

   a. *Promote the equitable distribution of wealth within nations and among nations.*

   b. *Enhance the intellectual, financial, technical, and social resources of developing nations, and relieve them of onerous international debt.*

   c. *Ensure that all trade supports sustainable resource use, environmental protection, and progressive labor standards.*

   d. *Require multinational corporations and international financial organizations to act transparently in the public good, and hold them accountable for the consequences of their activities.*

11. Affirm gender equality and equity as prerequisites to sustainable development and ensure universal access to education, health care, and economic opportunity.

   a. *Secure the human rights of women and girls and end all violence against them.*

   b. *Promote the active participation of women in all aspects of economic, political, civil, social, and cultural life as full and equal partners, decision makers, leaders, and beneficiaries.*

   c. *Strengthen families and ensure the safety and loving nurture of all family members.*

12. Uphold the right of all, without discrimination, to a natural and social environment supportive of human dignity, bodily health, and spiritual well-being, with special attention to the rights of indigenous peoples and minorities.

   a. *Eliminate discrimination in all its forms, such as that based on race, color, sex, sexual orientation, religion, language, and national, ethnic or social origin.*

   b. *Affirm the right of indigenous peoples to their spirituality, knowledge, lands and resources and to their related practice of sustainable livelihoods.*

   c. *Honor and support the young people of our communities, enabling them to fulfill their essential role in creating sustainable societies.*

   d. *Protect and restore outstanding places of cultural and spiritual significance.*

IV. DEMOCRACY, NONVIOLENCE, AND PEACE

13. Strengthen democratic institutions at all levels, and provide transparency and accountability in governance, inclusive participation in decision making, and access to justice.

   a. *Uphold the right of everyone to receive clear and timely information on environmental matters and all development plans and activities which are likely to affect them or in which they have an interest.*

b. *Support local, regional and global civil society, and promote the meaningful participation of all interested individuals and organizations in decision making.*

c. *Protect the rights to freedom of opinion, expression, peaceful assembly, association, and dissent.*

d. *Institute effective and efficient access to administrative and independent judicial procedures, including remedies and redress for environmental harm and the threat of such harm.*

e. *Eliminate corruption in all public and private institutions.*

f. *Strengthen local communities, enabling them to care for their environments, and assign environmental responsibilities to the levels of government where they can be carried out most effectively.*

14. Integrate into formal education and life-long learning the knowledge, values, and skills needed for a sustainable way of life.

a. *Provide all, especially children and youth, with educational opportunities that empower them to contribute actively to sustainable development.*

b. *Promote the contribution of the arts and humanities as well as the sciences in sustainability education.*

c. *Enhance the role of the mass media in raising awareness of ecological and social challenges.*

d. *Recognize the importance of moral and spiritual education for sustainable living.*

15. Treat all living beings with respect and consideration.

    a. *Prevent cruelty to animals kept in human societies and protect them from suffering.*

    b. *Protect wild animals from methods of hunting, trapping, and fishing that cause extreme, prolonged, or avoidable suffering.*

    c. *Avoid or eliminate to the full extent possible the taking or destruction of non-targeted species.*

16. Promote a culture of tolerance, nonviolence, and peace.

    a. *Encourage and support mutual understanding, solidarity, and cooperation among all peoples and within and among nations.*

    b. *Implement comprehensive strategies to prevent violent conflict and use collaborative problem solving to manage and resolve environmental conflicts and other disputes.*

    c. *Demilitarize national security systems to the level of a non-provocative defense posture, and convert military resources to peaceful purposes, including ecological restoration.*

    d. *Eliminate nuclear, biological, and toxic weapons and other weapons of mass destruction.*

    e. *Ensure that the use of orbital and outer space supports environmental protection and peace.*

    f. *Recognize that peace is the wholeness created by right relationships with oneself, other persons, other cultures, other life, Earth, and the larger whole of which all are a part.*

As never before in history, common destiny beckons us to seek a new beginning. Such renewal is the promise of these Earth Charter principles. To fulfill this promise, we must commit ourselves to adopt and promote the values and objectives of the Charter.

This requires a change of mind and heart. It requires a new sense of global interdependence and universal responsibility. We must imaginatively develop and apply the vision of a sustainable way of life locally, nationally, regionally, and globally. Our cultural diversity is a precious heritage and different cultures will find their own distinctive ways to realize the vision. We must deepen and expand the global dialogue that generated the Earth Charter, for we have much to learn from the ongoing collaborative search for truth and wisdom.

Life often involves tensions between important values. This can mean difficult choices. However, we must find ways to harmonize diversity with unity, the exercise of freedom with the common good, short-term objectives with long-term goals. Every individual, family, organization, and community has a vital role to play. The arts, sciences, religions, educational institutions, media, businesses, nongovernmental organizations, and governments are all called to offer creative leadership. The partnership of government, civil society, and business is essential for effective governance.

In order to build a sustainable global community, the nations of the world must renew their commitment to the United Nations, fulfill their obligations under existing international agreements, and support the implementation of the Earth Charter principles with an international legally binding instrument on environment and development.

Let ours be a time remembered for the awakening of a new reverence for life, the firm resolve to achieve sustainability, the quickening of the struggle for justice and peace, and the joyful celebration of life.

IF YOU WISH

TO BE INCLUDED IN OUR EMAIL LIST

---

*Please send the following information
at the web address listed below.*

NAME _____

ADDRESS_____

CITY _____

STATE _____   ZIP/POSTAL CODE _____

COUNTRY _____

EMAIL _____

www.RedwoodsInstitute.com

To place your order for additional copies, please visit us at:

www.RedwoodsInstitute.com